P9-ELX-707

SURPRISINGLY HAPPY

SURPRISINGLY HAPPY

...

An Atypical Religious Memoir

...

SHEILA PELTZ WEINBERG

White River Press
Amherst, Massachusetts

Surprisingly Happy: An Atypical Religious Memoir

First published March, 2010

White River Press
P.O. Box 3561
Amherst, MA 01004
www.whiteriverpress.com

Book design by Rebecca S. Neimark, Twenty-Six Letters
Front cover photograph: author, ca. 1953, Sylvia Glickman Dance Studio, Bronx; photographer unknown
Printed in the United States of America
ISBN: 978-1-935052-18-0

Library of Congress Cataloging-in-Publication Data

Weinberg, Sheila Peltz.
Surprisingly happy : an atypical religious memoir / Sheila Peltz Weinberg.
p. cm.
ISBN 978-1-935052-18-0 (pbk.)
1. Weinberg, Sheila Peltz. 2. Rabbis—United States—Biography.
3. Rabbis—United States—Anecdotes. I. Title.
BM755.W3573A3 2010
296.8'344092--dc22
[B]

2009039197

For Maynard
Thank you for everything

Table of Contents

Amherst, Fall 2009

I am counseling a young rabbinic colleague on the telephone. He says to me: "Do you mind if I ask you a personal question?" I say, "Go for it!" He says, "Are you happy?" I pause. I want to give him an honest answer. I say, "Yes, I am happy. I am certainly happier than I have ever been in my life." "That's interesting," he offers, and then poses another query: "Do you think you are happier because you are just getting older and that happens naturally or do you ascribe your happiness to spiritual practice?" Good question. "Frankly," I reply, "I have seen plenty of unhappy older people. Of course getting old can mellow you out, but in my experience happiness comes from practicing a view of life. It comes from working with my own mind and heart. It comes from feeling more at home in my own skin. Happiness is directly connected with how worthy I feel I am—how connected I feel to something greater than myself."

This book is about getting older and getting happier. It is the story of looking for God as I understand God, the God of a Jewish baby boomer, spiritual seeker, recovering alcoholic; a feminist grandma who loves yoga and is a rabbi. It is a series of snapshots along a life journey. You might see these snapshots as dots in the child's game of "connect the dots." We do not really know until the end what the final picture is supposed to look like. Each snapshot becomes clearer and more developed as it is lived, received, and ultimately left behind.

The Jewish mystics say that God is clothed in garments of concealment. Direct divine light would be too much for limited beings like us. Our task is to become strong and clear enough to see past the garments to the light and love that is forever streaming through us and around us. A contemporary mystic, Abraham Joshua Heschel, asks, "How do we become aware of God's presence in our lives, of God's passionate and compassionate concern for us?" These stories, snapshots and reflections are my response to that question. It makes me happy to share them with you. Perhaps you have a similar question in your heart.

Make Me a Sanctuary and I Will Dwell in Your Midst (Exodus 25:8)

How do I sit with that intention?
When I am far away, how do I return?
Where are the colors to lead me to the place
Where God dwells?
Where love and creativity abide?
Where no fear, no hatred, and no greed exist?
Where is the blue, the purple,
the crimson?

Rowe, Massachusetts, Spring 2003

I saw a workshop advertised in the Rowe Retreat Center Catalogue and I said to Maynard, "How would you like to go to a weekend workshop with Grace Paley on writing and politics?" He said, "Grace Paley? She must be pretty old. She is a great writer. She has always been a strong leftie activist. I bet it would be very interesting." "Terrific." I was thrilled. We signed up to go to Rowe, which is in the mountains of northwestern Massachusetts about an hour from our home.

The workshop itself was held in a big, drafty barn, with peeling paint and hard chairs. Lots of people were crammed in. Everyone left their shoes outside. My feet were cold. Most of these people were used to going to writing workshops and brought their manuscripts to receive guidance. Grace was tiny and majestic, wearing a huge grey sweater and sweat pants. Her hair was wisps of grey. She was in her 80s, a cancer survivor, pure energy, who gave total attention to each person. She seemed to know a lot of the women in the hall. Maynard was one of only a couple of men.

Friday night Grace Paley spoke about how her stories and her politics were inseparable and invited a few people to share their work. At the close of the session she said, "I am really interested in the stories you have not told. Think about what stories are waiting for you to tell. Tomorrow we will hear some of those stories."

Maynard and I returned in the cold and starless night to our room. While I was getting into my pajamas I turned to him and said, "I have a story that I have not told, about my brother, Chester. He died before I was born, but though I knew that, no one ever talked about it. I used to sneak into my father's drawer to look at Chester's picture." I felt pressure on my heart as I spoke.

Maynard looked at me with his kind eyes and said, "This is a perfect opportunity. You can tell the story tomorrow."

"I really don't think so."

He was insistent. "You must do it."

"I don't know," was all I could say before climbing into bed.

Next morning, Maynard practically pushed me up in front of all the writers and Grace Paley to tell my story. I am fine in front of people. I have been a congregational rabbi; I get energy from an audience. Still, I had never told this story. I felt open to the questions and comments and to the assumption that this would be a narrative I would write. Grace Paley was very encouraging.

I did write a few pages in Rowe; I put them into a folder in a dark corner of my study and forgot about them.

I want to write about Judaism and spirituality, about how I have been teaching meditation to rabbis, about the integration of meditation practice and prayer. I want to write commentaries of Torah rooted in the insights of meditation. I want to write about social justice and spirituality and the inextricable link between contemplating creation and experiencing liberation. I want to show how each of the Jewish holidays and Shabbat, indeed each Jewish prayer, is a teaching of mindfulness. I want to write about God as I understand God.

When I do sit down to write, I write stories—of course, stories, beginning with the story of Chester. Stories are the stuff of spirit, wisdom, transcendence, mystery. Humans are the species *narrativis*, the storytellers. Stories link the generations.

When I was little my mother told me a story about when her mother came to America. My mother's mother's mother packed a huge basket of fresh baked bread. My grandmother was leaving Bialystok for America and knew she might never see her mother again. The two women cried into each other's arms for a long time. They cried a river of tears. The tears went into the bread basket. When my grandmother opened the basket later that day on the ship, the bread was soggy and salty from her mother's tears and her own.

When I hear this story, I am no longer a separate little girl. I am part of this immigrant experience. I am part of the love of women, the grief of separation, the sweetness of those tear-drenched loaves of bread.

Stories straddle all the worlds. They are grounded in the particular and the unique: my story, my life, my experience, my family, my community. The Torah is mostly stories of the Jewish people. Stories also reach into the depths of universal life experiences—temptation, rivalry, love, faith, doubt, leadership, journey, liberation. All sacred texts are rooted in time, place, culture, and context. Yet they all drink the same water of life and breathe the air of this planet. They all cope with the failings and triumphs of human beings.

The narratives in the *Big Book of Alcoholics Anonymous* chronicle experiences of vastly different individuals finding freedom from suffering in unique circumstances. I listen to someone's story and I identify with it, even though the details are radically different. Sometimes I enter your story and discover a truth of my own. All literature counts on this. Stories reveal truth, not scientific truth but heart truth, truths of loss, return, freedom, and healing.

Sometimes stories reveal painful truths. Another favorite story of my mother's was about the day my Uncle Louis was born. My mother's mother Fruma came from Europe with her firstborn, a girl, Leah, renamed Lillian in the new country. Lillian was three years old when they arrived in New York and were reunited with my mother's father Samuel. A year later another girl, Ida, my mother, was born. According to my mother, Fruma didn't want any more children because she was afraid she might have another girl. The second girl was not greeted with great joy in this typical Jewish family of 1907. A few years later, however, Fruma became pregnant again. She was planning to have an abortion. Samuel woke her one night to tell her he had a dream that the child would be a boy. She agreed to carry the pregnancy to term. The day my Uncle Louis was born, according to my mother, was the happiest day in her parents' life. "It's a boy!!! It's a boy!!!" my grandfather screamed with delight from the stoop of their tenement in Harlem.

This is a story that carries a psychic wound of patriarchy. Multiply it by every story of rejection, exclusion, and oppression—all the stories growing scar tissue from the beginnings of time. The painful stories unite us too. They may invite a bonding that is tender enough to offer the balm of awareness. They may provide the scaffolding upon which to build a solidarity movement of liberation. Jews retell the wound of Egyptian bondage every day and every year as a catalyst to the ongoing project of personal and social liberation.

But not all stories liberate or heal. Not all stories inspire reconciliation or lead to solidarity. Some stories prop up my obsessions or delude me and keep me locked into cycles of hatred and resentment. Some stories call me into battle with my own shadows that I project onto another. Some stories trap me in confusion, greed, and violence.

Most stories do not fall neatly into one category or another. They invite me to ask myself where is the truth, light, healing, joy, compassion, the energy, the connection in this story, in my reaction to this story. Where is the aversion, the fear, anger, hatred, sadness, separation, judgment, confusion in this story, in my reaction to this story? Where is God hiding in these stories, in daily life, in resistance, struggles, relationships, twists and turns of choice and chance? Where is the light hidden—the light that was concealed in all matter after creation, the sparks of the divine? I ask these questions to create space to wait and listen. I do not need to do anything with these stories. The stories will reveal me to myself. The stories will reveal everything.

The story of Chester is important for me because it softens my heart, especially toward my father. I recognize in his gruffness, anger, and repression an effort to control and adapt to overwhelming grief. His anger was a condition of my childhood. It is stored in my cells. When I tell the story of Chester, compassion rises in my heart toward my father. His anger was not meant for me. It was the best response he could muster in a world where he felt helpless as a father to protect his children. I can embrace him or allow the God filled with mercy, *el maley rachamim*, to be my surrogate.

The fact that I was born in 1946, after one and half million Jewish children were killed, is not a random detail for me. I see anger and hatred as one Jewish reaction to the powerlessness of not being able to protect our children. I don't like the response but I can understand it. Unfortunately, the outer trappings of power—army, state, wealth, education, leadership—do not restore a sense of real power after such great loss. I see alienation from a God of mercy. A God of mercy after the Holocaust? You must be kidding! The only God we know is absent! I see spirit-seeking Jewish souls of my generation wandering to the far reaches of the East to hear a message of compassion that might restore balance and ease suffering.

Awareness of the Holocaust has been my companion since birth. Its story lives in my bones. Over the decades, many other terrible stories have joined this narrative of hate, all signaling the potential for depravity in human life. These stories rely on the illusion that violence will not contaminate those who perpetrate violence, that we can throw away what we do not like or what we fear and it will not return to destroy us. But there is no "away." There is only this present moment, this planet, this interweaving of life. There is only this, *zot*, a word for the Shechinah, God's indwelling presence. This is the story I want to tell.

Saying Kaddish for Chester, Winter 1945

My father, Marvin,
Crosses the Grand Concourse to go to Schiff Center
For *Shacharit*
So he can say *Kaddish* for his only son, Chester,
Dead at six years of age;
Hit by a truck on 170th street, in front of my mother's store,
In sunlight.
Every morning at Schiff Center,
Rabbi Abrams, short, compact, smooth face, straight gray hair combed back from his forehead.
My father, round face, black eyes, heavy beard, big belly. Always neat, starched shirt, tie, shoes polished.
Smoking Pall Malls. No filters.
A gold Masonic ring on his pinky.
What does he do with the pain?
Whom does he talk to?
Does he stay strong for Ida and Lorraine?
Does he ever see anyone beyond Chester? The boy's exquisite face, creamy skin, thick black hair, dimples, diamond ebony eyes (he looked so much like his father)?
Does he ever see anyone beside Chester's broken little body?
Does he cry?
Does he scream?
Does he hate God?

He walks across the Grand Concourse for morning *minyan* with Rabbi Abrams, Abba Abrams. His wife, Eleanor, calls him "Rabbi." Even at home.
My father is 40 years old.
In the middle of the war.
In the summer of 1944, the supply of xyclone B gas is being depleted in Europe. The cost of killing a child, two fifths of one cent, is deemed too costly.
Thereafter, children are thrown alive into the crematorium.
We teach: An image of God is of infinite value. Each life equals an entire world.
I am born in 1946, after the war. After one and half million Jewish children are dead, killed by the Nazis.
My mother tells me that she feels God punished her for not being a good enough mother by taking away her perfect boy.
When I am born, she knows God has forgiven her by sending this perfect little girl to her.
But what about Marvin?
Who punishes him and who forgives him?
His shell grows thick.
His voice grows silent.
Except when hot rage close to the surface breaks out.
He finds pleasure where he can—cigarettes, the stock market, television, eating late at night in his boxer shorts, driving his Oldsmobile.
Jews also grow a thick shell after 1945.
Thick with success, with a state, an army, universities, philharmonics, lots of buildings, lots of food.
Amazing that Marvin gets up every day, goes to work, comes home six days a week.
On Sundays we drive to visit my sister and her family in

the suburbs; we bring bagels, cream cheese and nova from the Bronx.

In the car he smokes, listens to the ball game. I am nauseous in the back seat from the smell of gasoline and tobacco and the sound of the announcer speaking a foreign language.

Amazing, too, that Jews build synagogues and schools, publish scholarly texts, prayer books, create courses, start summer camps and youth groups.

More than six decades pass. Babies become grandparents.

Questions abide.

Kaddish Poem

The *Kaddish* is about opening the window
Not looking through the glass, but opening the window.
The window of the heart, the window into not knowing.
Opening the window on fear and love.
Opening the window on time and space—*l'olam ulolmei olmeia*.
Just that.
Opening the window
To the kingdom that is just this.
Opening the window to the name. The great name.
No name.
Amen.

Avinu Av Harachaman Hamrachem Racheym Aleynu

Merciful father
To all the fathers,
May God have mercy upon them.
May we have mercy upon them as they seek their way into mercy,
Into love, into kindness.
Lord, have mercy,
All merciful Father,
Upon the fathers.
Let them turn their hearts to Yours
And find their way to You.
For You are always with them,
Merciful one.

Finding the Picture of Chester

I only got a few things when my mother died. I got an oil painting she copied from a picture of Jerusalem, very blue and gold. Pretty good. I hung it in my blue bedroom. I got another painting she and my father bought in Israel. It is a marketplace and the dominant color is turquoise. My mother liked that color. I painted the wall in the living room turquoise and hung the picture there.

I also got some of my mother's jewelry. She thought a man should buy his wife gold jewelry as a sign of affection. I never had a husband or boyfriend who bought me gold—silver if I was lucky, but never gold. I got my mother's gold sunburst with rubies and diamonds, matching pin and earrings that she wore on special occasions. I got a few odds and ends including a gold chain, a gold and diamond ring and a gold heart with a pearl in it that my mother's boyfriend Ira bought her years after my father died, when she was in her 80s and having a great time. The last piece was something I remembered my father buying for my mother. It was a $20 gold coin with gold rays coming out of the coin and little diamonds, hanging on a large gold chain. She really liked it. I could not bring myself to wear any of this jewelry except the ring. I couldn't sell it or give it away. Maybe Hadassah, my granddaughter, will like it some day.

I didn't take any of the books but I did take a few papers, including the certificate with Chester's headstone's inscription, signed by my father. It reads: "Shmuel Aryeh ben Moshe / Our Beloved Chester Lionel Peltz / May 16, 1938–November 30, 1944–14 Kislev." Then there are the initials in Hebrew meaning "May his soul be bound up in the bond of eternal life."

I also took a very brittle plastic case for small photographs. It had no cover and only three pictures. One was of my sister Lorraine. She looks about 18 years old. Her face was somber and she seemed to have a lot of lipstick on. One was a photograph of me at about four with my hair in ringlets, uniform long curls, wearing an organdy dress with a pinafore. The pictures were black and white but I think my dress was red. My mother thought that red was a good color for me because I was so dark.

There was one other picture.

I took these pictures because they brought me back to when I was little in the Bronx. Nobody ever mentioned Chester. No one ever said he existed or he is dead or that we ever had a brother, a son, a nephew, a grandchild. No one. Still I knew about him. Sometimes I opened my father's drawer in the greenish-silver wood bureau in his room.

The drawer smells cool, like wintergreen or medicine. I stand on tiptoe to open it. I know the plastic thing with the pictures is in there along with gold cuff links, tie clasps and those little white plastic things that go in the collars of my father's shirts.

My heart is pounding and I hold my breath, afraid someone will see me. I know it is not right to do this but I cannot help myself. I know who the boy is in the last picture. I know he is my brother. He looks like me; we have the same face, the same thick dark hair and large dark brown eyes. In the picture, he is wearing a little white shirt and a tie. I love him. I don't understand, yet I know everything. I will try to be good. I will try to do everything they want me to do. I will try my best. I replace the pictures and close the drawer. I breathe.

My Father's Mother's Diamond Ring, Purim 2006

I was in the kitchen and the phone rang. It was my son Ezra calling from Israel. "Mom, Olivia and I are talking more and more about marriage. Do you have a ring?"

Without hesitation I said, "Yes, I do." I hadn't given this ring any thought in decades but suddenly I remembered it was there, in the vault, a ring I could give Ezra to give to Olivia.

So the next day I went to the bank where I had a safe deposit box. My mother always called it "the vault." The young man from the bank accompanied me downstairs, where it was chilly and dark. He found the right box and we each put our respective copper keys into the locks. The box opened. There was a white envelope with blue handwriting on it. I recognized my mother's writing and it said "For Sheila, March 1962."

The ring was in a small brown leatherette box. The diamond was huge and gorgeous, sparkling and dazzling white light. The setting was simple and elegant. I took it with me and put the box back where it came from and called the same young man, who lumbered down the steps.

"Thank you so much. I got what I came for."

The ring belonged to my Grandma Peltz, my father's mother. From time to time, over the years, my mother would say to me, "Remember you have Grandma Peltz's diamond ring."

I have terrible memories of my Grandma Peltz, the other Ida Peltz. My mother hated her. I hardly ever saw her. When I did see her as a small child I screamed uncontrollably. My father never spoke about her. My mother told me that she once broke my father's nose and that was why he had sinus problems.

When Marvin, my father, was 18 years old, his father died. His mother was left with a teenage son and three young daughters, including one aged only two. While my father managed to get through pharmacy school at Fordham University, he could not fulfill his real dream, to go to medical school. His mother depended on him. (All his life my father hung around with doctors, loved to read about medicine and was a family paramedic of sorts.) Marvin was also very handsome and dashing. The girls didn't leave him alone. He was in his early 20s when he married my mother, who became the second Ida Peltz. His mother, the original Ida Peltz, cried so hard at the wedding (according to my mother) that no one could hear the rabbi speak.

Why did I have this diamond ring?

How did I even remember that I had it? Why didn't I ever take it out before? Why didn't I sell it or give it to my daughter?

Before Pesach, I took my Grandma Peltz's diamond ring to Jerusalem. On Erev Pesach, Ezra took Olivia to a spot overlooking the old city and asked her to be his wife. One year later they were married in Jerusalem. Four days later Olivia graduated from medical school.

There was something redemptive about giving the diamond to Olivia. She is a doctor. My father so wanted to be a doctor or to have a doctor in his family. She will be his legacy in that unfulfilled life. I can witness this and smile. The diamond can grace the finger of his grandson's wife as she tends and heals the suffering. I know it would make Marvin happy and that makes me smile.

My Grandma Peltz, a woman I feared and never knew,

was kept from a relationship with her sweet granddaughter for reasons I do not understand but can only imagine arising from old pain, wounds, feelings of unworthiness, and unloveability. Here is the diamond. It represents her wish to give me something of great value. Now I am finally able to accept this gift, which I immediately pass along to another as an act of welcoming, trust, and love.

Ramah and Ramaz, Spring 1955

"Marvin, the Abrams think Camp Ramah in Connecticut would be a great place to send Sheila this summer. It's run by the Conservative movement. Emmanuel went to their first camp in Wisconsin and now they are opening one nearer to us."

"She's only nine years old. Don't you think she's too young?"

"Not really. Lorraine was that age. It will be good for her. The fresh air, the swimming, the other kids."

So it was decided and I was driven to the Seminary on Broadway and 122nd street and loaded on a bus headed for Connecticut. It might as well have been the wilds of Alaska as far as I knew.

Over that summer my mother read an article, by chance, about Camp Ramah, discovering that they held services every morning and there were Hebrew classes every day. The counselors even spoke Hebrew to the kids. Most of the children were the sons and daughters of Conservative rabbis. My mother was not happy. But by that time it was too late. I had fallen in love with Hebrew, with trees, with the river, with the smell of the rain on the grass, with Shabbat. To me, they were all the same. They were all far away from Walton Avenue.

My father said to my mother, "Abba and Eleanor think we should send Sheila to Ramaz Day School in Manhattan. Emmanuel really likes it. It's a private school. She would get a great education in regular subjects as well as Jewish subjects."

"Absolutely not! There is such a thing as too Jewish. I don't want her to be too Jewish."

My mother had a very specific idea of the golden mean. In the area of being Jewish it definitely applied. You could be not Jewish enough, which was a big problem, such as eating non-kosher food or not going to shul on the high holidays. But you could also be too Jewish, which was equally serious. This was a grave danger for me. My mother told me, "Do your regular school homework first. Then do your Hebrew homework." I was a child in search of God, in search of goodness, succor, salvation, consolation, answers to the unknown questions, a refuge. I wanted to make up for my brother's death. I wanted to make up for the deaths of all the children. I wanted to make up for everything. Would someone please tell me the truth? Would someone tell me why it was so hard?

My Father and the Torah, Summer 1989

There is a huge pink granite building on the Grand Concourse and 169th Street in the Bronx. Today it is a Baptist church. When I was growing up it was a synagogue called Adath Israel, and my parents were members. I went to Hebrew school there. There were very few girls in the class, and I was a star pupil because I studied Hebrew at Camp Ramah all summer. I loved Hebrew school, even though the boys made the girls miserable. In the winter they threw snowballs at us; in the spring they squirted their water pistols; and in the fall, they tried to write on our clothes with pastel chalk. In the summers, I was back at Ramah, thank God.

The synagogue was enormous inside. The pews had red velvet cushions. There were white marble pillars on a giant *bima*, or stage. The words "Know Before Whom You Are Standing," in Hebrew, were etched in gold on a gleaming marble arch over the area where the cantor stood. The rabbi seemed insignificant next to the cantor. Cantor Mario Botachansky had a small goatee and wore a foot-high velvet and silver hat and velvet robes. (I never knew a Jew named Mario and no one I knew had a beard in the Bronx in those days.) Above him, out of view behind an opaque screen, was the choir, with the highest voices I ever heard. My mother called it *kvitching*.

The ark contained a dozen or more torahs, all sizes, with silver crowns, velvet mantles, purple and gold embroidery.

My father always fell asleep during services. I was afraid someone would hear him snoring. Sometimes I had a laughing fit for no reason at all and I couldn't help it. I liked to play with the fringes of his *tallis* on Rosh Hashanah or Yom Kippur. My parents never went to shul on Shabbat morning because the store was open and they had to work, but we did go on the high holidays and on Friday night. Then we came home for tea in special china cups and saucers with blue cornflowers. My aunt and uncle were usually there. Lots of times the rabbi, who was my brother-in-law's brother and was still single, came over too. (My sister's husband, Paul, was a Reform rabbi.) We had special cake from the bakery. My father was on the board of the synagogue. I had no idea what that meant.

I left the Bronx, got married, and moved on, and the Bronx also changed. Most of the Jews moved out, to Coop City, New Jersey, Queens, Westchester, or maybe Riverdale. Blacks and Puerto Ricans moved into the neighborhood. Everything was different and Adath Israel was sold to the Baptist church.

My parents moved to Fort Lee, New Jersey, overlooking the George Washington Bridge. My mother told me that my father got one of the torahs when they sold the shul. It sat in the front closet, on the top shelf, wrapped in an old yellow linen tablecloth. My mother said, "Daddy got that torah for you, you know." No one knew I was going to be a rabbi. Or did they?

Years after my father died, I was moving from Philadelphia to become the rabbi in Amherst, Massachusetts. I would be the first full-time rabbi in a place where until the 1960s there were hardly any Jews. The Jewish cemetery in Amherst dates from the 1980s. I cried when I first saw it, it is so new.

I stopped in Fort Lee to see my mother, who said, "Now you can take the torah." I wrapped it in a blue and white *talit* and put it in my little car and drove it, with my children and my furniture, up to Massachusetts. It was a beautiful little torah, very clear black letters on white parchment, not heavy. Anyone could carry it around. I could lift it up in services when called for *hagba*, to raise the torah and open the scroll for all to see the words. I asked Emma, a seamstress in the congregation, to make a new mantle for the torah. Emma was a sweet, frail spirit who found her way to Judaism as an adult. Her design featured a maroon and lavender velvet tree with leaves of blue and green, all sewn together with silver thread. It was alive.

Now the little torah travels with me and other folks to retreat centers and borrowed spaces where Jews gather to pray and study. During the week it lives at the day school in Northampton, where the children read it on Mondays and Thursdays. It is a little bit of my father, the Jews of Adath Israel, and the Bronx. *Etz Chayyim He.* It is a tree of life, ever dying and being reborn.

Etz Chayyim He

It does matter what you cling to,
What you hold on to. Whatever you call it.
God, Life, Torah, Dharma, Wakefulness, the One.
When you truly connect, hold on, trust this,
Then all other clinging is revealed
As a shadow, a garment, an echo.

My Bat Mitzvah, March 6, 1959

I have no doubts that this is where I want to be and I am terrified. It is Friday night. Today is my thirteenth birthday. I am sitting on a mahogany and red velvet chair. The back is two feet above my head. My feet do not touch the ground. The chair is on the giant *bimah* at Temple Adath Israel. My hands are clammy and I am freezing. I am shaking with fear.

I am wearing the most beautiful dress in the world. It cost $30 and my mother and I bought it at Saks Fifth Avenue in Manhattan, where we never shop. It is dark green paisley print, with a wide skirt, a scoop neck, and short sleeves. It hugs my rib cage, under my breasts. Green velvet ribbons crisscross the bodice to look like lacing. I am wearing stockings and little black pumps with small heels. The dress is itchy.

I insist on having this bat mitzvah even though there had only been one other one in this synagogue. The rabbi says I can do it on Friday night because we don't take the torah out then, so I (a girl) won't be called up to the torah, which would be against the Jewish law. I am not allowed to lead the service or chant the *haftorah* (prophetic portion) for that Shabbat. But, I may choose a different *haftorah* to chant and write a speech which I may read. This is fine with me. I choose the Book of Jonah, which is read on Yom Kippur afternoon (never at anyone's bar mitzvah), because I had studied it at Camp with a fabulous teacher. I study the cantillations with the principal of the Hebrew school. It is extremely long.

I am sweating and freezing at the same moment. I touch my face with my hands and they are like ice. Finally, it is time.

I know all the words and all the notes of the *haftorah* by heart. I warm up a little. Looking out, I see that there are a lot of people—kids from public school and Hebrew school, my sister and her husband, though they never come to the Bronx, my father's sisters, other relatives, my parents' friends, people from the neighborhood and the shul. Mrs. Davidson, my nanny since I was one, whom I call "Day," is there. She is Scottish Presbyterian, now in her 60s, with white curly hair and very fair skin, thin lips and blue eyes, stout and very kind. I still go to her house every year to see her Christmas tree and eat real Scottish shortbread. She loves me very much even though I don't need her to be my nanny any more and have not been so nice to her lately.

The speech is typed. I love this speech. It is about God and faith and the impossibility of running from God's presence. Jonah thought he could run away, but the whale swallowed him and spewed him out in exactly the place he was supposed to be. Most of all I love the fact that God gives us a chance to repent. No matter who we are, even citizens of the evil city of Nineveh, it is always possible to be forgiven, to be released from our cruelty, our confusion, our ill will. It is always possible to be brought back to God, no matter what the circumstances of our birth are. No matter our rebellion, no matter our falling away and falling down. No matter!

I love this. I am flying, soaring in mid air. I am scooped off the *bimah* at the end of the service. I am glowing. I feel as if I am exactly where God wants me to be.

Senior Prom, June 1962

I have two dilemmas during my senior year in high school. One is who is going to ask me to the prom? The other is how do I go on a Friday night? My senior year in high school is the pinnacle of my Sabbath observance. It dims and glows more brightly over the years and then it dims again. I am always in some relationship with the Sabbath. To me it is the supreme spiritual practice. It honors the majesty of creation as it celebrates the eternal possibility of liberation. The Sabbath, like all great spiritual practices, is a steady reminder of something important that I tend to forget.

In the fall, on the subway, Ed asks me if I will go with him to the prom. Ed is my friend. We ride home from school every day together. He comes to the youth group where I am the president. This attracts a group of girls because he is very cute, with beautiful dark blue dreamy eyes ringed with dark lashes and dark hair that he wears slicked back. He wears expensive clothes and plays the guitar. He is handsome and nice but I do not think of him as a boyfriend, and I do not want to go to the senior prom with him.

Ed is willing to go along with all my Jewish activities. He even comes with me to Manhattan to be in an Israeli dancing group that I lead. We eat out in the luncheonette on the corner of Madison Avenue and he gets a pack of cigarettes out of the machine. We light up. We are sixteen.

I tell Ed that I am not sure about the prom. I need to think about it. What I mean is I am hoping someone more desirable will ask me to the prom. Every week Ed asks me if

I have decided about the prom. He really likes me and will do anything for me. It's a bit much. I find it hard to respect someone who likes me this much.

Finally I realize I have to tell Ed I will go with him. He is thrilled and I am reconciled. Now I have the bigger problem: the prom is on a Friday night. Even though the school is more than 50 percent Jewish, no one seems to care. If there are Orthodox kids, they are pretty invisible and not about to make a scene. I consider myself an observant Conservative Jew. I am taking classes at the Jewish Theological Seminary. I am at a point in my Jewish religious life where I will not ride on Shabbat. I am firm about it.

The prom is at the Waldorf Astoria, all elegance, silk and champagne. But the Waldorf is in Manhattan, not walking distance from the Bronx. I talk this over with my parents, who talk it over with each other. They do not really understand my religious fervor but they really want me to be happy.

They have an idea. This is what we do:

My mother takes a room for us at the Waldorf. My father drives us down on Friday and then goes home. We check in. It is as elegant as I imagine. The room is tiny but the bedspread is red velvet brocade. The towels are thick and fluffy. I have a dress which is yellow and white organdy that I bought at Alexander's, on sale. Still, it looks good. The day before the prom, Ed and I had gone to Orchard Beach and I am still beet red. So is he. The dress's spaghetti straps cut into my sunburn, but I don't care.

We light Shabbat candles in the room when Ed comes. He is wearing a white dinner jacket with black pants and a black tie. He looks great. He is so happy. We go downstairs to the prom, which is terrific. We eat, we dance, we even go to a club afterwards. We walk in Central Park with other couples in the moonlight, feeling like we own New York. When Ed brings me back to the room at the Waldorf, it is close to dawn. He goes back to the Bronx. Around noon on Saturday, he comes down again by subway. My mother takes the train home. Ed and I spend the day in Central Park. It is June and very warm. We listen to music, watch the people and talk until the stars come out. Shabbat is over, and we go back to the Bronx on the subway.

Petach Tikvah, September 1962

In Camp Ramah, I learned to dream about Israel, the place where the Jews could really have a free, safe body, in a land that smells of oranges and eucalyptus. I remember the cover of Theodore Bikel's album *Songs of Israel*, which I got when I was about 15. It had a picture of a strong, tanned, smiling Jewish girl with thick braids, wearing khaki short shorts walking through a field of alfalfa. I would play that album over and over again.

When I was 16, I begged my parents to let me go to Israel for a year on a program called the Institute for Youth Leaders from Abroad. My mother was reluctant but I was unrelenting in my appeals. We said our teary goodbyes at Kennedy Airport (Idlewild in those days). My Uncle Louis said, "Remember, every day will be long, but the year will be short."

Israel in 1962 was a spare place. There was no television, no tuna fish, no peanut butter, no traffic, no East Jerusalem, no Wall, and no West Bank. I couldn't call home. I wrote aerogrammes with a ball point pen, scrawling flowery prose into the little flaps of the thin blue paper.

I checked into our dormitory in Jerusalem and was told after a few days of orientation that I had a week of *chofesh* (free time). This was daunting. I didn't know anyone in Israel but I did have a list of names and addresses given to me by my Aunt Lilly. She had kept up a correspondence in Yiddish with my mother's Israeli family after my grandmother died. Lilly was also our only relative to have visited Israel, a year or two ago. I decided to visit these relatives.

First I go to the bank. It is *hamsin* in Jerusalem. The dry winds are coming off the desert in waves of hot exhaust fumes. No one had told me about wearing a hat or drinking lots of water. I am in the bank line, and suddenly I am lying on a vinyl couch and people are fanning me with newspapers. I had fainted. When I revive, I promptly purchase a *kova tembel*, a fool's hat. This is a classic Israeli cotton hat that fits on the head like an upside down soup bowl. Mine is light green. I make my way to the Egged bus station and ask for a seat on the bus to Petach Tikvah. I have no idea where that is but it is one of the places where my relatives live. Thanks to all my years at Camp Ramah and Hebrew school I am completely fluent in Hebrew, although I have a strong American accent.

I manage somehow to change buses in Tel Aviv and make it to Petach Tikva. I wander the dusty streets asking for the address written on a now crumpled piece of paper in my hand. My *kova tembel* is glued to my head by sweat. I buy an army canteen and fill it with water, which I keep sipping. It is getting dark. I turn a corner and find myself on the right street. The house I am looking for is small, painted pink, with a broken white fence. I ring the bell and a boy about my age opens the door. He has my face. Tears start to roll down my cheeks. I have found them. I explain who I am and a whole group of people, adults and children, surround me, call me in, embrace me, and sit me down to feed me salad and white cheese, rolls and butter and tea.

My program had many facets. We spent half the year studying in Jerusalem—Hebrew, Israeli history, literature, geography—all with a strong Zionist flavor. There were Jewish kids from all over the world. I mostly hung out with the American kids I came with. We came from United Synagogue Youth, which is not a Zionist group but is part of the Conservative movement in the U.S. The other groups were either

Orthodox or not at all religious, like my relatives, who were surprised that I was kosher and didn't want to travel to go to the beach on Shabbat. I found it all very confusing.

Another part of the year we lived on a religious kibbutz. I worked mostly in the kitchen washing dishes. My hands turned red, rough, and calloused. I loved the kibbutz—the green geometry of the alfalfa fields, the smell of jasmine. I even loved the smell of diesel fuel from the tractors and motorbikes. I loved the kibbutz family that adopted me. I loved eating tomatoes and cucumbers for breakfast in the vast common dining room. I loved Jews farming the land of Israel. I loved polishing the little brown leather shoes when I got to work in the children's house.

I did not love the synagogue. A high curtain separated men and women and most of the women don't even bother going to services. Again, I felt confused and stopped going to services. I no longer knew if I was religious or not. There seemed to be no place for the Judaism I learned at Ramah. I was not sure what the point was of being religious in Israel when it was all Jews and all Hebrew all the time. I started smoking on Shabbat, the cheap unfiltered Nadiv cigarettes that we got for free from the kibbutz. We joked that they were made of camel dung. I was too exhausted on Shabbat to do much but sleep in the hot afternoon.

Part of our year, because we were in a "religious" group, included a month in a yeshiva in Jerusalem. It was May and *hamsin* was back. I came to class in a sleeveless cotton shirt, and the teacher made me leave; sleeveless was not allowed in his all-girls class. He spoke sharply to me, his voice filled with judgment. I felt deeply hurt. I went back to my room to change and hot tears welled up in my eyes. I was furious and confused and full of resentment. If this is what religion is about, I didn't want to be religious. I was hot and tired and I missed my mother.

I wanted so much to belong, to know who I am and what God wants of me. But it was not easy. Sometime that year, on a little card I wrote this advice given by the poet Rilke and hung it on the wall over my bed: "to have patience with everything unresolved in your heart and try to love the questions themselves as if they were locked rooms or books written in a very foreign language. Don't search for the answers, which could not be given you now, because you would not be able to live them. And the point is to live everything. Live the questions now. Perhaps then, someday far in the future, you will gradually, without even noticing it, live your way into the answer."

Coming home from Israel was not easy either. I went back to living with my parents in the Bronx and they were not getting along very well. I commuted to City College by subway. I was a freshman and my friends from high school were a year ahead of me. I acquired a bad cold and a cough that lasted seven months. JFK was shot and I felt as if I had lost my closest relative. I was overcome with grief. My Jewish studies at the Seminary were boring, beside the point, parochial. I dated men I didn't like. I decided I needed to get away from everything and applied to transfer to the University of Chicago. That was as far removed from the Jewish world as I could imagine.

In April, I met Steve. He had a head of dirty blonde curls, a dimple in his chin, and a Vespa motor scooter. He was from Scranton, Pennsylvania, on scholarship at Columbia. He was the oldest of four siblings. I thought that was cool. We had a lot in common, both of us passionate, idealistic and adventurous. We wanted to join the Peace Corps and make the world a better place. On our first date he took me to a Shlomo Carlebach concert, and we stayed up until four in the morning talking. I was ecstatic. Then he didn't call me. For three weeks, I stared at the telephone. Finally my mother and aunt couldn't stand it anymore and said, "Call him!" I had two tickets for the World's Fair in New York and two tickets for Richard Burton playing *Hamlet* on Broadway. I called him and asked him to go with me. He said, "Sure."

At Rachel's Tomb, Bethlehem

Who am I to weep at the
Supposed grave of a
Dead ancestor?
Yet, tears fall—thick and sweet—at your
Blue velvet bier,
Beloved Rachel,
While outside
Boy soldiers, in green,
Stand guard.
Tears for them
And for me
A great flowing river of tears.
Yours, Rachel, remembered
For so long
And mine, still fresh,
Mix with the tears of all the mothers,
And overflow,
For a moment,
The dry banks
Of separation.

Columbia University, April 1968

I flew to Chicago in September 1964 but my heart remained on Morningside Heights in New York. I called Steve from the phone booth in my dorm while the other girls waited their turn. He got a drive-away car on the weekend of Election Day. The day Johnson beat Goldwater, I lost my virginity at the YMCA in downtown Chicago, wearing a wedding band I'd bought at Woolworth's to show the girl at the front desk.

We had plans to work together at Camp Ramah during the summer of 1965, but another opportunity arose. Steve, a campus leader, received a grant to run a pilot project called Double Discovery. This was the dawn of the short-lived War on Poverty. Promising kids from poor families were invited to spend the summer at Columbia with great teachers and enriching New York experiences. Steve was the program director and wanted me to be one of the counselors. I was thrilled. We shared the dream; I had been tutoring poor kids on the South Side of Chicago. The Ramah director was furious with me when I told him my plan. He chastised me for making a foolish and unethical choice. I was hurt and felt confused and betrayed. I could not understand why he didn't see that what we were doing was a fulfillment of everything I learned at Ramah. I never returned to Ramah.

Steve and I lived in a fraternity house near campus. I taught swimming. We took the kids to the Statue of Liberty, Coney Island, Hyde Park, and the Metropolitan Museum of Art. There were riots in Watts that summer, but we felt that we were making a difference. Meanwhile, Steve made more money than he ever had in his life and bought a Honda 90 with his first month's check. I was disappointed; I had hoped for a diamond ring. For me, it was important to get married if you were in love, especially if you were having sex. Steve didn't really want to get married, but I convinced him. With his second month's pay check, he went to Tiffany's and bought a white gold engagement ring with a small round diamond. I returned to Chicago with the ring but I did not last the quarter.

For the first time in my life I was flunking a course, Physics. I couldn't concentrate. I told my parents I wanted to drop out of school. My father was furious and flew to Chicago to beg me not to do this, but I did it anyway. Steve and I got married in January. My father walked me down the aisle biting his lip.

I was back at City College, but this time I could walk there. Steve had one more semester at Columbia. We taught Hebrew School to support ourselves.

The Vietnam War was heating up. Steve applied to graduate school to get a draft deferment. We stayed in our apartment, which was at eye level with the Broadway train where it went above ground, right before 125th Street. Every time the train passed by, it was harrowing. But it was a great apartment, and we loved it. I graduated from City College and took a one-year master's degree in teaching at Columbia. All we talked about was the war. Our friends were being drafted. We went on marches to the Pentagon and to New Hampshire to campaign for Gene McCarthy. I wanted Steve to burn his draft card. We talked about moving to Canada. There were more riots. I watched the news every night, seeing the body bags, the draped coffins, the napalmed children. I felt tremendous guilt, rage, and fear, but no doubts; I knew at the core of my being that this was wrong. I also knew that those going to the war were poor and black, uneducated, chosen but not choosing. This too made me furious. I was privileged and I was ashamed of my privilege. I smoked dope and listened to the Beatles with Steve and our friends.

The night Martin Luther King was shot I smelled the tear gas from our apartment window and heard the police cars going after the looters.

One afternoon in April, we were on our way to New Jersey to teach Hebrew School when Steve told me there were students sitting in at Avery Hall where his Urban Planning program met. It was all part of a takeover of several campus buildings in response to two main issues. One was the encroachment of Columbia University on its primarily poor and black neighborhood, taking away homes to expand labs and offices. The other was the connection between Columbia and an institute implicated through funds and research with the war itself. I was aflame; my heart was pounding. The war on poverty and the war in Vietnam had both landed on our doorstep. I knew what we had to do—no deliberation, no doubt, only action. I never talked or thought about God; I no longer considered myself a religious Jew. But in this moment, I felt like I was being called to something greater than myself.

Steve and I spent three days in Avery Hall, eating peanut butter sandwiches and sleeping on the floor, not changing our clothes. We held strategy meetings and got reports about what was happening at Low Library. We learned about student protests in the streets of Paris. It looked as though the new world was breaking through. It felt like we were at the center of the universe.

On the third day rumors started to fly around about the police. The leaders told us to gather on the fourth floor of Avery. I looked out the window and saw a lot of people outside. But they couldn't be police. I thought of police as men with dark blue shirts tucked into dark blue pants, with gold buttons and thick leather belts. Police wore hats with brims, like airplane pilots and officers in the army. But these men were wearing chinos and knit shirts; some were wearing button-down shirts and ties, and some had khaki or light blue poplin jackets on. They weren't wearing hats. Some of them were talking into small black devices.

The students were sitting down in one room on the floor in a circle. We linked arms. Someone started to sing "We Shall Overcome" and everyone joined in. I heard noise, the sound of heavy, running steps. The men in khaki slacks and knit shirts broke into the room and started to handcuff us, dragging us out. Steve and I were handcuffed together and they dragged us down four floors. The asphalt was cold and very hard and my wrists hurt. I was terrified but relieved that I was with Steve. They threw us into a police wagon and took us to the city jail.

In the morning my father came to post bond and to drive us home. I was very happy to see him, but he was unsmiling. That night, Steve and I went to Shabbat dinner at my parents' apartment in the Bronx. In late May, we appeared before a judge to sever our case from the rest of the students so that we could join the Peace Corps. It was a draft deferment.

Puerto Aisen, Chile, September 1968

Hubert Humphrey got the nomination in Chicago the summer Steve and I studied Spanish in New Jersey. In September we left for Chile with a group of urban planners, some with their wives, who were also Peace Corps volunteers. The program was meant to bolster Chile's central government by adding staff to the regional urban development offices up and down thousands of miles of Chile's length. We were sent to the southernmost post, Puerto Aisen.

We took a plane from Santiago to Puerto Mont, in southern Chile. This is where the Pan American highway ended and travel continued only by boat or air. We boarded a very small plane. The door sounded like it was not quite shut and rattled frantically during the journey through the clouds further south. We arrived at an airstrip in Balmaceda, which had one small, unpainted wooden cabin. From there it was a three-hour ride to Aisen on unpaved, muddy, rock-strewn roads. Our new home was a room in the Hotel Aisen. Over the next few months, we became aware of the phased demolition of the hotel while we were still guests.

No one in town was quite sure why we had come or what we were supposed to be doing here. I found it a frightening place, with packs of wild dogs roaming the streets day and night. It was always cold, rainy, and foggy. There was no heat and our luggage never arrived. The urban development office in the municipality was on the second floor of the municipal building. We climbed a ladder to get there, but the toilet was an outhouse in the rear. They used old municipal memos for toilet paper. Fruits and vegetables rarely got to Aisen; instead, the locals ate shellfish and potatoes, and so did we. They drank a lot of very cheap wine, and so did we. We never knew what would be for sale in the general store in Aisen; it depended on the boats that were passing through. Sometimes the store was filled with rubber boots, sometimes batteries or blankets.

In Aisen I often ran into Germans who lived on the islands hidden in the fog, days' sails away. I chatted with them from time to time in English. They assured me that they were on the Russian front in World War II. Americans must like that. I never mentioned that I was Jewish. There were lots of rumors about Nazi war criminals who were hiding in these parts.

I got a lot of reading done waiting to find out what to do. I read *War and Peace* in the first two weeks.

Steve and I left Aisen after four months and made our way to Santiago where many of the other Peace Corps volunteers had congregated, streaming to the capital from their posts. I ended up teaching in a Catholic school. There were no books and fifty or sixty kids in a class and I was completely unprepared. We hung out with other volunteers and smoked a lot of grass. One volunteer brought a laundry bag filled with local weed from the north. Volunteers from other parts of Latin America arrived with their stash, from Panama and Colombia and other spots. I was frightened, and the pot did not help my fear. I was scared by the dogs. Crossing the street terrified me, as drivers did not seem to pay attention to the signs. I was afraid of getting a terrible disease from the food or the water.

It was confusing to read in the local paper that the Peace Corps volunteers were being accused of being spies. "How ridiculous!" I thought to myself. This ragtag group of draft dodgers and hippie wannabees fancied ourselves radicals. We marched on the American Embassy in Santiago on Moratorium Day, 1969, to end the war in Vietnam.

Years later, I learned that this was the heyday of American covert operations in Chile, before Allende's election. I have wondered from time to time if anyone in our group had worked for the CIA.

Steve and I traveled to Peru, Bolivia, Argentina, and Brazil. I started to get interested in pre-Colombian civilization, as I realized that the kids were being taught European history, made to identify with the Spanish Empire. It was like leaving Jewish history out of the history of Europe or asking Jews to identify with the Roman Empire or the papacy. Why were there no books about indigenous cultures and the pre-Hispanic civilizations? I decided to write a textbook on the Americas before Columbus. One of the volunteers was interested in doing the illustrations, and we had a great time with this project. I wrote in Spanish, on a new mission to give history back to its owners. I was enraged and grief-stricken as I read about "la conquista," but I was also exhilarated by this work.

Then I got sick—really sick. I couldn't move. I had fever and no energy and more anxiety, and I couldn't eat. The Peace Corps doctor didn't know what to do with me. Eventually, I got a diagnosis: typhoid. When I read the warning label on the medicine I was even more terrified. One of the primary side effects was death! I thought I was going to die and would never make it back to the U.S., never see my mother again. I did not know it but at that very same moment my mother was undergoing surgery for colon cancer. We hid our illnesses from each other.

I tried to get out of bed and the room started to spin. Was it the illness? Was it my fear? I couldn't tell. I was emaciated. I went into the hospital for some tests: nothing. One of the

Peace Corps staff told me I had an anxiety syndrome and offered me Librium. Half the volunteers were offered Librium for our various ailments. I refused to take it. I had a better idea: I wanted to get pregnant. If I got pregnant I would live, for I would have a reason to live. I wanted something to believe in, something to love. I wanted something greater than the small world that was closing in on me.

I was about four months pregnant with Abby when we landed at JFK. I was wearing a loose-fitting short navy blue dress and my belly was still pretty small but round. My hair was long, pulled back with a rubber band. There were huge dark circles under my eyes. I hadn't slept in about 24 hours. I saw my mother from a distance and started to run. I was running and sobbing because I had thought I would never see her again. I was so grateful to be back.

Steve would be 26 in October, the magic age for Selective Service. He also got a fairly good number in the lottery. In July he would be a father. We didn't have to worry any more about the draft.

Jerusalem, Yom Kippur 1973

Steve, Abby, and I were living in Scranton. He had a job as a city planner and I was teaching part time. There was nothing the matter with our life but I was not happy. I blamed Scranton, but Steve said it was me. I got ideas about where we should go. I had put my entire Jewish and Zionist life on hold. I felt as though I had put my professional life on hold. I was restless and bored and I needed a dream. I wanted to travel. While I might in theory value contentment above discontent, I have to admit that discontent in my life sometimes fuels the next step of the journey—the next dot along the way of the follow-the-dots drawing. I find myself propelled forward toward the wholeness and wisdom that is forever emerging.

We talked about moving to New York or California and settled on making *aliyah* to Israel. I wanted a real Jewish life, but not Orthodox. I could not abide the secondary role of women. I could not wear long sleeves in the *hamsin*. I didn't see other options in America. I may not have believed in God, prayer, or religious practice but I did believe in the Jewish people. I believed in Jewish survival, which loomed as the greatness I aspired to be part of. I believed in Jewish destiny and for me, Israel was where it was at. This was what I wanted for my daughter.

I loved teaching but I was bored teaching junior high. I wanted to teach college, to become a professor of Jewish history in Israel. I reasoned this out and it all made perfect sense to me. We could apply for assistance to the Jewish Agency to become immigrants. We could buy a car in Europe and travel for three months and then take a five-day ferry from Marseilles to Haifa. We could enroll in an absorption center to study Hebrew and find work and a permanent place to live. Israel was eager for Western immigrants and Israel would help us make this plan work.

Steve agreed, although he said, "I am willing to bet that this won't make you happy. I want to be clear that after three years if either of us is not happy, we are coming back to the U.S. and we are coming back to Scranton."

We followed our plan. We bought a white Peugeot 404 in Paris and drove though France, Switzerland, Italy, Spain, and Portugal. Gas, food and lodging were very cheap in Europe before the October War. We visited a lot of playgrounds. I have a picture of Abby wearing green plaid wool overalls, sporting two shiny black pigtails, playing on the grass in front of the Prado in Madrid. I don't remember ever getting inside the museum. That was the kind of trip it was. We ate a lot of ice cream and hunted for toilets. We finally ended up in Marseilles with immigrants from Morocco on their way to Israel. We arrived in Haifa on Hanukkah, 1972, and headed for the absorption center in the hills outside of Jerusalem. It was a quiet moment in Israel's life, a time of temporary relaxation and unwarranted optimism.

Things moved along. I got a job at Hebrew University that might lead to a doctoral program. Steve had a job. We put a down payment on an apartment. Abby was in nursery school and was looking and speaking like an Israeli. We had a few friends, mostly Anglos, recent arrivals.

Yom Kippur, 1973: we had the day off, hanging out at home and listening to music. Our apartment was in French Hill, in a very new high-rise complex to the north of the city, in the part annexed to Greater Jerusalem after 1967. We were listening to Judy Collins as Abby took a nap in her crib. We were listening to a song about whales. Our American neighbor knocked on the door. "Do you hear the sirens?" "What are you talking about? It's just the whales from our record. We will make it softer." "Look out your window!!!" We looked out and saw bumper-to-bumper Egged buses heading north on Damascus Road. On Yom Kippur, there should be no traffic in Jerusalem. We realized that those were air raid sirens and we saw our other neighbors, especially the Russians, scurrying downstairs to the bomb shelter. I went into the bedroom and scooped up Abby with her blanket and bear, sweaty with sleep, and headed downstairs.

Given the history of the Jewish state it sounds silly to say we were utterly unprepared for war. But that was the truth of it; we were unprepared. Some of the men were shining their boots while waiting for mobilization orders. Several of the women admitted that their husbands had been gone since before dawn. The news was frightening and confusing. Someone had a short wave radio, and we heard that Israel has been attacked by Egypt and Syria—we didn't yet know about Jordan. We got instructions about stockpiling water and blackouts. Our own building was a potential lighthouse for enemy airplanes striking Jerusalem.

This war changed a lot. Steve lost his job because everyone in his department was called up. Israelis were very depressed, and there was a lot of talk about leaving the country. Shock gave way to shame and dread. We had no role to play; Steve was not in the military. I felt guilty and embarrassed to have my husband around. The post-1967 euphoria had crashed around us, and idealism itself sounded suspect. Israelis laughed when we told them we had come on *aliyah*. We missed our families more than ever. All our friends were talking about going back. My father was ailing. My parents made one more trip to visit us in the spring, but I knew it would be

Marvin's last trip. He ended up at Shaare Tzedek Hospital with wounded soldiers crowding the corridors.

Looking for something helpful to do, I discovered that families were needed to house volunteers from abroad who were coming to Israel to help. We volunteered to host some of them. A month or so after the war, our guests showed up: Phil and Sue, sweet young Americans from the Bay area, both fair and very slender. They enjoyed chatting with us and playing with Abby. One evening the conversation turned to drugs. Phil asked us if we had ever tripped on acid. We both said, "No, why?" It turned out that Phil had more than enough blotter acid to turn us all on, at least once. "Were we into it?" It would be his way of thanking us for our hospitality.

Steve was thrilled and had no qualms. I was scared to death. I imagined revisiting my anxiety syndrome. My resistance was not prudish; I simply had no confidence that my trip would be anything but a disaster. But Phil was persuasive, assuring me that he would be there for me and that there was really nothing to worry about. For some reason, I did not want Steve to do it without me and he was determined to do it. "It's a great opportunity." Very reluctantly, I agreed.

There are many ways I could describe the one and only time I ever dropped acid. I could tell about the music, the color, the sense that time was moving ever so slowly. I could tell how we go out to the neighborhood Arab grocer and I see the most beautiful man I have ever seen in my life. I fall in love with his smile. I could say it is an experience of revelation. My right brain comes alive. I am not caught in judgment, fear, desire, or any other left-brain function of separation and discontent. I am firmly rooted in unity. I see and understand that God is always. God is not something or someone separate to whom one pays homage. God is alive at this moment in this room, in this body, in this flower. God lives in the chaos and the order, in the darkness and the light. I see that there is a possibility of having access to this vision. I have no idea how but I now know it is part of the repertory of my humanity. Nothing will be the same. A seed is planted in my consciousness that will change the trajectory of my life. Out of the depths of the disappointment and tragedy of that Yom Kippur a new way of seeing is born for me.

Scranton, Passover 1975

We came back to the US for Rosh Hashanah 1974. I was pregnant. My parents sent us a ticket for the holidays. We left everything in our apartment in Jerusalem. Steve got a new job in Scranton and returned to Jerusalem to sell or give away our stuff. I resigned my job and the prospect of a Ph.D. I am disoriented; I don't know what is happening. When our son is born, I name him Ezra after the priest in the fifth century BCE who led the return of the Jewish people to their land after the Babylonian exile. It is my guilty protest for having abandoned Israel. Ezra means "help." When he is born I am crying for help from God: "Help me find my purpose." I really was praying when I named that baby Ezra.

When Ezra is a few months old, I am introduced to a group run by an extraordinary teacher, David Brahinsky. David and his wife Naomi are friends of ours and we have children the same age. David and Steve share a birthday. David is a short compact man with riveting dark eyes and a bushy beard. He knows that I am searching. He encourages me to read a book by Ouspensky called *In Search of the Miraculous*, about Ouspensky's teacher Gurdjieff. The book awakens the part of my being that hungers for meaning and connection with the infinite. The meetings I attend, led by David, are even more remarkable. I sit in an old barn with 20 strangers and feel the presence of something sweet, soft, embracing. At the same time I feel totally alive and real. David talks about the difference between essence and personality. He suggests that reality or truth is much more layered, dynamic, and profound than the external levels of our lives. My experience of being in the group is vastly different than reading a book. I actually feel that I have an essence that is pure of personality, unconfused, free of fear, turmoil, and sadness. David was my first spiritual teacher. His very being transmitted his teaching. The group did spiritual practices together, mostly meditative movement and dance. David spoke about waking up from our sleep of unawareness, stopping to identify with every feeling, thought, and role. He taught liberation.

I began to feel certain that I had found my purpose in life. The call for help had indeed been answered. I felt an electric current lighting up my insides. I wanted to embody these teachings and teach others. I would devote time and energy to this work. I realized, however, that I must do this work as a Jew, for I was certain that the same ideas and approaches to life existed in Judaism. Suddenly shock waves ran through my body. I could become a rabbi and teach about waking up in the language of my own ancestors. I knew in my heart that these teachings are deep within Judaism, despite the fact that the local synagogue feels utterly devoid of spirit to me.

On Yom Kippur eve, I walked out in the middle of services and drove to David's barn to be in an environment of true longing for transformation, of working on oneself, as Gurjieff's followers call the process of liberation. Years later I learned that the Kotzker Rebbe calls Hasidism *arbeit auf zich*—working on oneself.

I started reading voraciously. I read Heschel, Buber, and Mordecai Kaplan, who clearly understood about waking up. Jeffrey, a Scranton friend who was studying to be a rabbi at the Reconstructionist Rabbinical College in Philadelphia, came over whenever he was in town. He told me that I should think about being a rabbi. He told me that the smartest person in his class by far was a woman. Art Green and Zalman Schachter were living in his neighborhood, Mount Airy, and I would love to study with them. All kinds of interesting and innovative Jewish things were going on.

Jeff invited Steve and me to his graduation from RRC. I was in tears when two women walked down the aisle to become rabbis. The graduation speaker was Rabbi Harold Schulweis from California. I felt as if he was speaking personally to me. He spoke about the function of religion in our lives and how we have mistaken the external forms for the inner heart and soul of Judaism. He explained how Judaism is meant to be a transformational practice that turns our fears and struggles into a path of goodness and connection. I was on the edge of my seat. I have never heard anyone speaking so directly and so clearly. I felt overwhelmed. I rushed up to the rabbi at the end of the graduation and waited while others had words with him. Finally it was my turn. I thanked him for his talk and blurted out: "I am going to be a rabbi." He nodded politely at my exuberance.

Mount Airy, Elul 1977

The first time I saw the Germantown Jewish Centre, it looked like a mountain, rising high above Lincoln Drive, a grey stone monolith. You entered it not from Lincoln Drive but from around the corner. There are two entrances on Ellet Street, one into the main sanctuary (it was years before I ever went in that way), the other, a more modest door, near the playground. It opened to show grey cinderblock walls and beige marble asphalt floor tiles. I entered it with my children. Abby was seven, great dark eyes, shiny long curls, plump cheeks, a little messy. Ezra was two and a half, just out of diapers, with a runny nose and long hair. He was impossible to keep track of, constantly looking for a way to have fun. Abby held my hand.

I was 31 years old, newly divorced and just moving to Philadelphia. Steve and I stayed married for eleven years. We had our adventures. We loved our children dearly, but we were both immature. Conflict, poor communication, hurt, guilt, disappointment, anger, agendas, all piled up on top of one another. We wanted each other to be different. We had very limited skills as partners. We separated and went our own ways to different cities and communities, dividing our friends and our few possessions. The divorce was not congenial and created more misery. We could not divide our children.

I had been told there were alternative Shabbat morning services at Germantown Jewish Centre, all reached through this one entrance. We went up the stairs, turned left down the dingy corridor and then left again through a door and down a flight of stairs. We found a room with gray metal seats in a circle. A few people sat on the floor on a shaggy blue rug. A man of about forty with grey hair, a beard and a sweet face was leading the singing in a melodic voice.

There was something about this place that reminded me of Camp Ramah. In fact, I had moved to this neighborhood in particular because of Rabbi Jeff and because of an article I read in the *Jewish Exponent* about West Mount Airy and this alternative prayer service called the *minyan*. I felt immediately at ease and at home in a place I had never been. I joined the singing, keeping one eye on Ezra.

After a while some folks got up and moved a table into the center of the room. There was a small torah on the table covered by a *talit*. A woman a few years younger than I was, with very long straight brown hair pulled back with a rubber band, now took charge. She looked strong and confident, not thin but compact and wore dark pants and a sweater. Over it all, she wore an enormous wool *talit*, gleaming white with black stripes. It was so large that it trailed on the floor, even though she had draped it around her shoulders. She read torah in a loud, clear voice. I had never seen anything like this before—a woman wearing a *talit*, a woman in charge of a service. For all those years at Camp Ramah, only boys were allowed to wear a *talit* and only the boys were allowed to read from the torah or lead the services. I never thought anything of it; it was just the way it was. But now my soul glowed. Things would never be the same.

Eight years later I decided it was time for me to have my own *talit*. I had gradually gotten used to wearing ones that belonged to the shul or to someone else. When I saw my friend Devorah's *talit* I knew this was what I wanted. I connected with the designer, a local artist named Rita, a short stocky woman in her thirties with a round face, gleaming skin, bright eyes, and electric energy, a singer, an artist, a healer, a dancer. I felt lit up in her presence, something that was a little scary. Rita said, "Sure, come to my place and I will show you the kinds of material you could use and you can think about the design you want."

When I arrived at Rita's apartment, she pulled out an assortment of fabrics, mostly silk, but some cotton, some wool. All were white or beige. She encouraged me to try them on, to feel them. There was one heavy silk fabric that felt amazing, cool and light and comforting. I said, "Rita, this is it." Then she said, "What is your idea?" I said, "I want a rainbow. I want my Hebrew name. I want this poem that I love about the grass and the sky. I want peace, shalom, all around it."

This was at a time in the 1980s when I was active in the anti-nuke movement with Arthur Waskow and the nascent Shalom Center. We spoke about the rainbow as a symbol of coexistence, pluralism, and peace. It was during Reagan's presidency, in the last gasps of the Cold War.

"What colors do you want?"

"I want all the colors, the whole rainbow."

Rita got to work.

I came back in a few weeks and there it was, my *talit*. I loved it. There was a lot of pink in it, but also purples and greens flowing into each other. The rainbow was there but without sharp definition. The separate colors swirled into each other through the batik process, hot wax and Rita's magic. The silk felt cool and soft. My name was there in chartreuse Hebrew script, Harav Shulamit Devorah bat Moshe v'Chaya. It anticipated graduation from rabbinical school.

Rita and I tied white wool fringes (*tzitzit*) to the four corners with the appropriate blessings. The knots in the *tzitzit* are a code for the name of God. The name cannot be pronounced. It stands for breath and being and becoming. The name, like the *talit*'s fringes, ties together the multiplicity of created things and affirms connection, relationship, wholeness.

When I graduated from rabbinical school, my friend Arthur and his partner Phyllis gave me a new set of *tzitzit*, dyed every color of the rainbow.

I wore this *talit* for 25 years. I wore it on the *bimah* (pulpit) in Philadelphia and Amherst, where the 12-year-olds got their parents to set up a workshop to make tie-dyed *talitot* for their *bnai mitzvah*. I wore it at an interfaith yoga, meditation, and dance workshop in Steamboat Springs, Colorado, and one of the participants, a Roman Catholic priest, danced with my *talit*. I wore it at anti-nuke and save-the-planet demonstrations. I wore it when I said kaddish on the railroad tracks at Birkenau. I wore it on February 15, 2003, when I was on the podium for the New York rally to stop Bush from invading Iraq. I wore this *talit* in my room at Insight Meditation Society when I sat with the prayer book every morning before joining the community meditation in the big hall. I wore this *talit* when my son was called to the torah before his wedding in Jerusalem. This *talit*, attached to tall branches, was the *chuppah* (canopy) at weddings where I was the rabbi. It was the *chuppah* when Maynard and I got married. It wiped away a lot of tears over the years, absorbing the sweet saltiness better than any Kleenex. I planned to be buried in this *talit*.

My *talit* was a garment that concealed and revealed. It revealed a woman owning her spiritual equality with men after millennia of patriarchy. It concealed resistance to being just like the men. It was a new garment, fashioned for a breakthrough moment—self-conscious, a little gaudy, but soft and resilient. When I wrapped myself in my *talit* I could say anything I wanted to God.

On my way home from Detroit via Philadelphia in March 2008, I checked two bags. One had the clothes and books I had schlepped to lead workshops and then to visit my daughter and granddaughter. The second bag was a smallish black backpack with my favorite pillow that traveled with me for the sake of my neck, other odds and ends, and my *talit*, in an old blue velvet bag, crammed with random *yarmulkas* and pieces of paper with prayers, teachings and songs. There was an eight-hour delay in Philadelphia due to weather. I got home very late. The black backpack did not. Every day I checked with the airline but it was not coming. Finally they told me that it was officially lost. They had no idea where it was. I was sad, but not *that* sad. In fact I was surprised I was not sadder. The truth is, I was ready for a new *talit*. I was ready to honor the power of that sacred shawl. I was so grateful for the road we had traveled together. But I could also begin to imagine what a new *talit* would be like.

The *talit*, like Shabbat, is a spiritual practice. It is an object in space rather than in time, reminding me of something important that I am likely to forget. Jews call spiritual practices *mitzvoth* or commandments. I see them as vessels, earthy containers that hold our aspiration to align with that which is greater than our separate self. We pour our intention into a day or a garment. We make an effort to remember— what? The unifying source from which all arises, the flow of love that fills all creation, including our own little corner, never disconnected from the whole.

Drinking and Getting Sober, Memorial Day Weekend 1987

There was a liquor store on 170th Street, part of the family business. The day Prohibition ended, my uncle stood in line and got a license. On Christmas and New Year's Eve, the store stayed open late. Business was great. My father and uncles were working. I hung around and ate corned beef sandwiches. When my Uncle Louis picked my mother up from her store after work, sometimes he shared a miniature with her. Those were little bottles of all kinds of liquor. We never drank at home. On Sundays, after visiting my sister, my parents and I went out to eat at the Clam Box. We ate fish—never shellfish, but red snapper, filet of sole, cod. My father would have a Manhattan and my mother a whiskey sour, just one each.

I loved martinis. I guess it's the olive and the shape of the glass. If you asked for a dry martini and you were lucky, you might get straight gin with the merest whisper of vermouth. I was 15 years old when I had my first martini. We were in a very fancy restaurant in Manhattan, having dinner "on" the carpet manufacturers. My father and uncle had greatly expanded the retail business in the Bronx. Masters' discount stores were opening in the suburbs, with departments owned by different companies. My father became friends with Steve Masters and decided to invest in a dozen stores or so—a big chance, a big risk. My mother was opposed to it. She hated borrowing money, big business of any kind, and risk. My father and uncle were dreamers and neither was a businessman. My Uncle Louis would have been a great college history professor and my father wanted to be a doctor. My mother was the only one who really loved business. She loved handling money; she loved the merchandise, and she loved selling. Even when she retired at age 70, she continued to sell. She sold anything to anyone to raise money for Hadassah or the shul.

I got to go to these fancy dinners, with incredible food. My mother started eating non-kosher meat. She reasoned that a really good filet mignon, even if it was not kosher, was as good as kosher. No one really noticed if I had a few martinis. I felt terrific. There was nothing to worry about. I was happy.

At Columbia, I developed a taste for bourbon. Since Steve was a campus leader, we were invited to receptions hosted by President Grayson Kirk. I noticed that Kirk was drinking bourbon. I figured, why not? Saying "bourbon on the rocks" made me feel beautiful, sophisticated, witty, and above all, worthy.

I never drank one drink. If I drank one, all I thought about was the next one. How could I get the next drink without looking like I was trying to get it? I wanted to get that feeling. I loved it. I lost my fear of people. I forgot that I am not as good as I need to be, or as smart, as pretty, as popular, as sweet, as thin.

On our honeymoon in Nassau, in January 1966, in the Bahamas, I learned how to make a bossa nova. I brought home all the ingredients: rum, apricot liqueur, pineapple juice, Galliano (it comes in a tall skinny bottle and is yellow) and egg whites. I put all the ingredients in the blender and the drink came out frothy, festive, and sophisticated and tasted great. I was thrilled and served bossa novas when we entertained and invited people for dinner. In fact, I invited people over so that I could serve bossa novas, which I drank before and after as well as during the meal. On our first New Year's Eve, we threw a party and I got so drunk that I spent most of the night throwing up in the bathroom.

I drank until I was 41 years old. For a long time, alcohol was my closest friend, my steadiest companion, my most dependable source of comfort and support. It sustained me in hard times. I believed in it. It was my refuge, my fortress, my stronghold, my secret. It was my golden calf. I drank the cheapest wine or the best scotch, whatever was available. The only thing I didn't like to drink was beer, unless I was desperate. By the time I was a single mother living in Philadelphia in 1977, I was almost a daily drinker. I had my standards though. During the week, when I was working, I didn't drink before 5. Then I came home to make dinner for my kids and filled a large coffee cup with cheap wine or vodka or gin. I didn't bother buying vermouth. I explained to myself that drinking gave me more patience with my kids, mellowed out my edgy temperament, and relaxed me so that I could be a better mom.

My drinking grew more and more hidden. For my daughter's bat mitzvah, I bought gallons and gallons of hard liquor. My friends and family drank a tiny bit and I kept the rest in the cellar. The cellar was scary to me; it was dark and damp, and smelled moldy, with cobwebs and mice that terrified me. I went down those creaking stairs every night to pour myself a drink from the half-gallon bottle of rye or vodka until the supply ran out.

I continued to drink through jobs, spiritual communities, women's groups, political work, rabbinical school, relationships with rabbis and doctors. Once I fell and broke a foot and once I cracked my coccyx. I was still drinking when I graduated and became a rabbi. The bartenders at the bnai mitzvah knew me. "What'll it be, Rabbi?" I ordered Chivas. I knew that I was an alcoholic and could not stop, although I tried. I had enough discipline to do two years of rabbinical school in one year while being the rabbi of a synagogue, in a long-distance relationship with a man, and raising two children as a single mom. But I could not stop drinking. I hated myself for this.

I started reading books about addiction and recognized myself. But no one in my life called me on this. I coped so well; I was such a great concealer. I tried to tell my women's group and their response was a chorus of "Don't be ridiculous, Sheila. So you drink. Look at you. You're terrific."

Memorial Day weekend, 1987: I have a horrible cold. I am working full-time as the rabbi of a congregation in Philadelphia. I write into my contract that I am off every Memorial Day weekend so that I can go to Bnot Esh, an organization I helped found. It is a group of Jewish feminist scholars, teachers, and activists who help to create Jewish feminism. It is a cauldron of personalities and passion. We meet at the same place every Memorial Day weekend from Thursday night until Monday morning. Different groups take responsibility for the program each time. We talk, study, eat, pray, laugh, dream about our lives, the Jews, the planet, women, men, children, growing up and growing old, money, violence, love, sex, God....

A day or two before, a friend of mine comes over with a bottle of bourbon. "Here's some medicine for your cold, sweetheart." "Thanks. Great." On the drive up on Thursday I feel lousy. I am achy and a little feverish and my throat is burning. It's harder than usual to sleep on Thursday night. It's always hard to sleep at Bnot Esh. There are four women in our room and there is so much to say and we laugh until we have to pee.

Friday is very intense, even for Bnot Esh. The subject is abuse, physical and sexual. Women are telling their own stories. One woman who has an alcoholic husband and knows a lot about alcoholism says something like, "You are as sick as your secrets." I feel as though a dagger has pierced my chest.

Something weird happens at dinner. There is always wine for Shabbat. I go to pour myself a glass and one of the women says to me, "Sheila, don't you know that's poison." The words are a neon sign in my mind. I pour the wine anyway and sit down next to a friend who I know has been struggling with her own addiction to pot. I take a sip of the wine and turn to my friend, "I have to tell you something. I really think I have a problem with alcohol."

In that moment the floodgates burst. I am telling someone who knows. She says, "Come on; let's go in the other room." We are sitting on cushions on the floor in the dimly lit wood-paneled meditation room. There is an oriental rug on the floor. I am wailing. Tears and snot are streaming down my face. It is all coming out. I am out of control, racked with pain. And in the midst of it all, I am speaking in sputtering sounds: "I understand. I can't do this alone. I must have help. I must have help. I must have help from God. I need to put this in the hands of God. This is what I have to do. I am so sick, but it isn't my fault and God will help me and there are people that will help me. You will help me, won't you? What should I do?"

I manage to get through the next two days. I tell a few of the women, ones I guess will get it. I tell my roommates. I am detoxing at Bnot Esh. I have the shakes. My vision is blurry. The floor is not quite under my feet. But I don't have a drink.

I get home on Monday. Before I pick up my kids I go to the kitchen at the rear of the house. I take the four-liter bottle of cheap white wine and pour it on the little patch of grass behind the house. My cat is looking at me. Then I take the bottle of bourbon and spill it out in the same place. Then I spill out a bottle of Kahlua someone gave me that I don't bother drinking anyway because the alcohol content is too low. I go upstairs and get the pipe, a bag of grass and some papers and stuff them in the outside garbage can. Then I get my kids.

"Come on up to my bedroom, I need to talk to you about something important." Abby is almost 17. She is pretty well aware of everything at this point and has been getting a lot of drug and alcohol education at school. Ezra is 12. I don't know what he knows. They sit on my bed. Their dark eyes are very wide open. "This weekend something really important happened. I recognized that I am an alcoholic. It is a sickness and I need help with it. The help will come from people who know about this and from the people who love me. I can't drink any more. It is a bad thing for me. I need to tell you this and I need your support. It will be really hard and I trust that God will help us." My voice trails off. Abby is staring at me. Her eyes get even wider. There is a pause. I say: "The most important thing I want to say is...." Again my voice trails off. My mind is not very steady. It is hard tracking thoughts. In the silence, Ezra looks straight into my eyes and says, "The most important thing is that we tell the truth." I start to cry and grab them both and hug them to me. It is going to be okay.

The next day I call the number of the drug counselor that my friend gave me. A woman answers and tells me that that particular counselor doesn't work there any more. I could call this other number. I call. It's a place in Center City called Oasis, providing alcohol treatment for women. I make an appointment for Wednesday. I find my way to the unfamiliar block and when I reach the office the receptionist tells me that the person I am supposed to see is not in. "Do you want to see someone else?" I am shaky. I am the rabbi of a congregation walking into an alcohol rehab center, for myself. What if someone sees me? That is the least of my concerns in this moment. I need help. "Yes, of course," I say.

A woman the color of a starless night moves toward me. She walks with power and strength and ease all at once. Her black skin is gleaming. She is smiling at me. "I am Faith," she says. Then she grabs me and gives me this huge bear hug. She smells of violets, lavender, honey, and cinnamon all mixed together. I will do whatever she tells me to do. I really want to get sober.

I have not had a drink or a drug since that night at Bnot Esh. I am still working on my sobriety.

Compassion

I stand in the center of the circle of shame and blame.
Around me pointing their fingers, wagging their heads,
scowling, screaming, they stand.
The carrots (the ones I cut slowly and unevenly this
morning),
The cook,
The teachers,
The books,
The other students who are all doing better.
"You should be doing better!"
"You should be feeling better!"
"You should!" "You're not!"
"Shame on you!"
Somehow I reach for the prayer book.
The words speak to me,
They speak of shelter and refuge.
They know.
You do not abandon those who seek you.
And I seek You.
That is why I am here.
Stumbling, stumbling over every rock and broken
branch along the way.
I am here to seek You.
You do not abandon those who seek You.
Then I find an old note a teacher gave me once
encouraging me to say these words: "Out of
compassion for myself, may I open to this pain,"

And of course,
You are here,
In this pain,
In the note,
In the open,
In the compassion,
In the teacher,
In the words
In the silence.

Amherst, June 2008

I have been out of town for a few weeks. It is good to sleep in my own bed. I wake up about 6:30, wash and dress quickly and walk up the hill into town. The day is already warm and the sky is clear. At the top of the hill I make a left, walk another block, and make a right. I head toward an apartment building. I enter the lobby and press the code on the key pad. The buzzer signals that the door is open. I go inside. Once on the elevator I press "five." At the end of the hall is the meeting. It has just started when I enter the room. Six men are sitting around a table covered with papers, books and coffee mugs. I smile at each one in turn. I know them all. A young slender blonde man is chairing the meeting and asks if there are any announcements. Mike says: "Yes, I have an announcement." He looks at me. "I would like to give Sheila her medallion for 22 years of continuous sobriety." I break into a huge grin. "Mike, I am very appreciative but actually it is only 21 years. Thanks for the add-on. I will make every effort to merit it. I can't believe how sweet it feels that you guys remembered my anniversary. I am really touched." Mike says, "Gee, I had 22 years written down. Keep that one and I'll get you another next time you come."

I have been sitting in rooms like this one for 21 years. While I was a congregational rabbi I went at lunchtime. Sometimes I went to evening meetings. Often the meetings were held in churches. For many years I went to the Newman Center at UMass. I sat in a room with a big crucifix and a bunch of other drunks for an hour—ex-cons, priests, prostitutes, professors, homeless men and women in half-way houses, physicians, artists, businessmen, teen mothers, crack and heroin addicts, pill poppers, women who sip white wine all day in their homes, Hispanics, Afro-Americans, Indians, white men, gay, lesbian, and trans, young and old. Human variety is infinite. So is the universality of suffering and the healing power of telling the truth and being heard without judgment.

I always come out feeling better.

I sit and listen to people talk. Sometimes I feel like I might go out of my mind if they don't shut up already. They trigger all kinds of feelings—anger, fear, impatience. Still, I just sit. I watch my own reactions. I try not to judge what is going on in me any more than I judge the speaker. The muscle of tolerance grows as the environment of safety spreads. Who knows when that very same person will say something that will help the jagged pieces of my life fall into place? I say things I do not say anywhere else in my life. People nod. I share my shame. I share my highest aspirations. I never know what I will share until I open my mouth.

I remember when Mike came into the meetings seven years ago. He was a powerful man with a beefy face, an athletic build, belly bulging over his belt. He was in his late fifties, just my age, with a broad Boston accent. He always had a lot to say. At first he complained about everything. He had lost his family and his career to his drinking and was living in a halfway house. His driver's license was suspended. He had health problems. His face is badly scarred from cancer surgery. He walked with an attitude. "No one seems to know how to get things done around here."

I watched Mike over the years. I watched him learn to listen and how to be grateful. I watched him open up to a power greater than himself as he talked about how he had to learn that he is not God—how he came to believe in Good Orderly Direction, an AA acronym for God. He talked about becoming less of a spoiled brat. Mike got incredibly active, starting new meetings, going to regional events, setting up a meeting at the VA hospital, sponsoring newcomers. He printed out all kinds of AA literature that he got off the internet for us. He became involved in local politics, advocating for low-income housing and public transportation, regularly visiting the State House. Everyone knew him. He did more than not drink; he stayed sober. He had a library of AA literature. Sometimes during meetings, I would look across the table and watch him underline in different colors certain words and ideas he wanted to remember. He scrawled notes in the margins of every pamphlet. He had a way of making the generalized concrete, taking it to heart. He wanted to make himself of use to something greater.

Mike was always there at 7 am, making coffee, putting on water for tea, setting out the literature for that day, often chairing the meeting. Even on the days when he was scheduled for chemotherapy, he made the coffee first. In the last year he started bringing his cat, "my spiritual advisor," to meetings. The black-and-white cat was comfortable walking across the table and snuggling up to any of us. Mike set up a bowl of food for him in the back of the room.

Mike spoke frankly about his poor health but his words were always surrounded in a frame of gratitude, joy, and responsibility. He modeled the serenity, courage, and wisdom that come from devoted practice. It was amazing. There was so much suffering in these rooms and there was so much hope. I always feel it when people say, "To hell with everything I have learned. All I really want to do is connect to something real—to tell you what is true for me—to ask for help." And they do.

I needed to travel again. When I got back I checked my email. There was a message from Rick, a member of the group who worked for an NGO in Africa and the only recovering

AA in the city where he was based. He came to the 7 am meeting in Amherst when he was home on leave. The rest of the time he communicated with us by email. Rick's email said, "I just learned of Mike's death and am filled with sadness. Let me know any further information. Love, Rick." I called another friend from the meeting and she confirmed that Mike died yesterday. She didn't know about a funeral or memorial service. There was an article in the local paper later that week. Other folks stepped up to the plate and started making coffee for the 7 am meeting. I was happy Mike gave me two years of medallions. I was surprised that I missed him so much.

The key to AA for me is safety. Of course there are social conditions that are necessary for any of us to feel safe: enough food, a safe place to sleep, security against violence, health care. These are the minimum conditions. But how much is enough?

How safe is it to be a living being anyway, even in the best of circumstances? When I focus on keeping this separate existence free from harm forever, I am fighting a losing battle. Only when my source of ultimate safety is my deeper connection to the whole web of life, can I feel held. It is then that I understand the meaning of the line in the Hebrew prayer, *B'yado afkid ruche*: "I put my spirit in your hand." I put my spirit in the hand of God who is revealed as One, concealed as many. AA is above all a spiritual program. Safety and spirituality go together.

I wonder: How do we create conditions to feel safe enough to allow the soul to be known? The soul exists, but it may be crowded out by judgment, noise, speed, competition, distraction, excessive stuff. I do know that by lowering the volume, I allow the soul's frequency to be heard. This, in my experience, is what is required for spiritual renewal, one soul at a time.

My Mother Hates Fatness

My mother hated fatness. I was a pudgy baby and a chubby little girl. My mother decided that she would not let me grow up to be fat. She limited what I could eat. She would give me half a jar of baby food instead of a whole jar even if I wanted the whole jar. She told me about this with pride when I was an adult. My mother's favorite phrase regarding food was "that's enough for you."

My mother equated being overweight with sin. Maybe she was trying to limit the space a female body took up. She had been taught that women inhabit a less worthy human form. My mother was also trying to protect me. She knew that a female is judged on her physical form, which determined her ability to attract men; hence her security hangs on her not being fat (at least in this culture). Above all, my mother wanted me to be safe. I understood that.

My mother ridiculed and reviled fatness in friends and strangers, even in characters on TV. Fatness was evil and weak. My father was overweight, and my mother harassed and chided him as he popped another cookie into his mouth. He would stay up late after she went to sleep, sitting in his white boxer shorts and undershirt in the dinette, eating and smoking Pall Malls and reading about the stock market in *Business Week*. This was his revenge.

I wanted my mother's approval and developed a fear of fatness. As a teenager I started to smoke cigarettes and drink coffee and diet soda as a way to keep my weight down. At first cigarettes made me nauseous, but I persisted until I smoked a pack of Kents a day.

In my 20s, after Abby's birth, my fear of fatness got serious. I stopped getting my period. Even my mother thought I was too thin and kept telling me that I looked like a survivor of a concentration camp. This was before anyone ever heard of anorexia. There is a photo in an old pile somewhere of a plate with a tiny piece of meat and a dozen green peas on it. Steve took the picture to show me how small the portion was that I took for myself. I was underweight, but I felt that I was too fat. I pinched the skin of my stomach with disgust. But I also loved sweets. I bought Archway cookies and ate three cookies at every meal. I ate little else—maybe a tiny bit of cottage cheese in the morning, the meat and peas at night. I cut little pieces of the cookies with a sharp knife and drank cup after cup of coffee (there was no decaf in those days) and smoked my Kents.

Like the drinking, the smoking and compulsive eating was harmful to my body. Yet it was a ritual I enacted to make me feel I had some authority over my body and my spirit. I thought: if I am thin enough, I will be acceptable, worthy. In a roundabout way, I was longing for Divine love, yearning to be acceptable in my humanness. But each cigarette distanced me from a feeling, a fear, a sadness. I became less and less alive with each drink that softened the edges of my mind. I believed I had the power. In reality my effort at control disconnected me from the vulnerability of being alive.

I need not abuse substances in order to cloud my mind and obscure the truth of my life. I do it with stories of resentment. I do it with fantasies of glory. I do it with obsessive thinking about past mistakes. I do it by judging myself and others mercilessly. We all do it in a million ways that keep us stuck in our captivity.

In Judaism, these are considered forms of idolatry. I placed my faith in beliefs and behaviors that promised to control my reality. I imagined I had power. But false gods rob me of the true power I do possess, the power to feel my own aliveness, to touch the experience of this moment as it manifests right here, right now, in this vessel. I forget and forego the intention to open myself to be the chariot for divine grace. This is how I understand the section in Exodus when the Israelites are restlessly waiting for Moses to come down the mountain. It says: "And all the people took off the gold rings that were in their ears and brought them to Aaron. This he took from them and cast it into a mold, and made it into a molten calf. And they exclaimed, 'this is your God, O Israel, who brought you out of the land of Egypt.'" (32:3–4)

The golden calf seems to me to be the paradigm of *avodah zarah*, false allegiance or misguided effort fueled by deluded thinking. I see my life as a journey to discover what is worthy of worship—what leads to true happiness and security. This is what I would call *avodat hashem*, serving the Eternal One. Judaism is a path full of sacred practices that help me on this journey. There are hundreds of practices, like saying blessings before enjoying the bounty of nature, immersing in the *mikvah* (ritual bath), eating *matzah*, dwelling in a *sukkah* (harvest booth), feeding the hungry, clothing the naked and visiting the sick.

It is also true that every truly conscious breath has the potential to be a sacred moment. I set an intention: "May this act allow me to feel alive with God's presence in this moment. May this act bring the eternal into time and the infinite into space." When I am able to sincerely set this intention, I am happy.

I am aware of the danger that practices, even ones from the ancient traditions, can be disconnected from intention. Then they can become dull, rote, brittle. I find myself going through the motions. The thought occurs, "Who cares? Why bother?" Or I am doing the action and thinking about last night or next week or who said what to me last. The pulsation between alive, luminous spiritual practice and empty gesture is part of the history of religion. It is part of my own journey. Even worse, religious practices can become so disconnected from aliveness that they become weapons of self-righteousness, arrogance, alienation, and even violence.

Ironically, I began to understand the potential of Jewish practice more deeply as I embraced spiritual practices from other traditions. In my 20s I studied karate. The teacher asked me to focus on a particular point in my belly where my power is located, inviting me to bring my mind, my imagination, into my body for a specific purpose. It was a revelation. Karate is not just a sport; it is not about winning and losing. It is about becoming a true warrior, integrated, and connected in mind and body.

Years later I became an avid yoga practitioner. Yoga means the yoking of heaven and earth. As I enter a pose I create the chariot, making an effort to align with something greater than myself. I make an intention to bring my awareness to the alignment. I open. I receive a flow of life hidden in the cracks and crevices of this body, sparks of divine light. The radiance of living spirit flows through my cells. I feel part of the whole, more capable to act with courage and commitment to my true values. I begin to learn that my body can be a vessel to contain God's love rather than a symbol of punishment and object of revulsion.

I wonder, "Could waving a *lulav* (a palm branch) and saying *kiddush* over wine be more like yoga? Could giving *tzedakka* (charity) and comforting the bereaved be a more deliberate path to awakening consciousness?"

Jews have a concept called *teshuvah* that I think is essential to any contemplation of spiritual practice. It means turning or returning. If these practices are supposed to help me wake up and remember who I am in the highest sense, what happens when I forget? I know from my experience that the mind will surely forget the intention, again and again. I will forget that everything in this world pulses with Divine light. I will look away. I will look down. My mind will tend to scold itself for this weakness. In the millions of times that this has happened, I have noticed that it is not helpful to scold my mind for forgetting. That is the way the mind is built and trained. What is helpful is the possibility of *teshuvah*, returning to the intention. The good news is that I can return no matter how many times I forget, fall down, or wander off. I celebrate this Jewish spiritual teaching every time I begin again—every moment, every morning, every new month, every new year. It is the gift of creation.

My life is a struggle between *avodah zarah* (idol worship) and *avodat hashem* (worship of God). It is my constant choice to embrace my humanness. It is my regular practice to open to something greater than my own tale of woe. When I do open, I become aware of how universal my own experience is. I open to the fragility and magnificence of this earth. I receive wisdom and clarity to act in ways that are loving, true and strong.

I want to tell you what I know: It is more and more urgent to love ourselves, each other and the earth, through our differences, to make life, especially for the weak among us, safer and healthier in the air, water, and earth. I know it is more and more urgent to help our children know the nearness of Divine love as they walk into the unknown. It is my experience that a renewed dedication to awakened spiritual practice will serve us well on this journey.

I wish the world a global Sabbath practice, a rest from harming our beloved mother, this planet, taking her into our hearts as she cradles us in her arms.

1478 Walton Avenue, Summer 1989

When my parents held the *mazel tov* party two weeks after I was born, the building where we lived in the Bronx, 1478 Walton Avenue, had a doorman. The brass was shiny. The inlaid brown and gold tile floor in the massive lobby glowed and the paint on the elevator was red and thick.

By the time I was a teenager, the doorman was long gone. The elevator broke down a lot. We had to climb the smelly stairs up to the third floor, where we lived. The red paint was peeling. There was a mirror in the inside corner of the elevator to see if someone scary was coming in so that you could run out.

Our apartment was across from the elevator. You entered what my mother called the foyer. She didn't pronounce it *foy-ay* as in French but *foy-er*. I didn't understand this room. It had no purpose, except that was where the telephone was, on a small black carved wood table in the corner next to the single chair. There was a large crystal chandelier hanging from the ceiling, made up of glass beads shaped like teardrops, golf balls, icicles.

To the left was the living room where we hardly ever went. My parents put wall-to-wall beige pile carpet throughout the whole apartment. Before that there was an oriental rug in the living room, smooth as velvet. When I was very small I enjoyed tracing the shapes with my fingers. Down the hall and to the left was the kitchen-dinette. Further down the hall was my parents' bedroom where they watched TV at night. To the left and around the corner, past the bathroom, was my room. My room had two windows, one facing Walton Avenue. In the summer I could hear the women who sat on the sidewalk in lawn chairs talking to each other late into the night. From the side window I saw a small asphalt-paved courtyard between our building and the next one, with one scrawny tree with an iron fence around it.

Our building had six stories and was built of brick, one in a sea of identical buildings as far as the eye could see. I used to think this was how the whole world lived. When I went out the front door, I turned left, passing PS 64, a brownstone fortress surrounded by a grey wire fence. I walked two blocks to 170th Street where "The Store" was—my mother's store. This part of 170th was crammed with stores—two kosher butchers, the lingerie store, the haberdashery, the liquor store, Casey's fresh fish store, the kosher delicatessen, the pizza place, the knishe joint, Woolworth's, Bartons Chocolates, the vegetable market, and much more. It stretched four blocks on either side from the Grand Concourse to Jerome Avenue, where the elevated Lexington Avenue subway ran.

My mother's store was Osherson's Floor Covering, but we just called it "the store." My mother's father, Samuel Osherson, started the business when he came to New York from Bialystock. His first store was in Harlem. When the Jews started moving to the Bronx in the 1920s my grandfather opened this store on 170th Street. In 1924, my mother was 17 and about to graduate from Wadleigh High School. She had planned to register at Brooklyn Law School, but instead she started to work with her father in his new store.

The store was long and narrow. On one side were the six-foot-high rolls of linoleum standing at attention. Some looked like wood, tile or marble; others were splattered with color, light or dark, pinks, blues, and grays for a background, with gold or silver flecks. Behind the rolls of linoleum were the rugs, nine or twelve feet tall, beige and green and dusty rose, shags, tweeds and piles, sculpted with leaves, flowers, or geometric shapes. On the other side of the store were books of carpet samples and boxes of tiles. There were a few chairs where my mother sat when she was not talking to a customer or arranging the window. When I was very young, my mother's mother was there most of the time. Fruma (Flora) spoke Yiddish and didn't read English so she couldn't write up an order. After she died, my mother's sister Lilly was often in the store, talking to my mother. She never waited on the customers. There were two men who worked there, Rudy and Ben. Ben reminded me of a mouse or a weasel, and I didn't like his looks. He was short and wiry with grey hair and a foreign accent. I liked Rudy better. He had dark hair and a pencil-thin black mustache and a nice voice, and he smiled at me. Many years later my mother revealed to me that Rudy had been stealing from the register.

In 1970 my parents moved to Fort Lee, New Jersey. My father retired but he drove my mother to and from the store every day. The neighborhood was now mostly Hispanic. There were bodegas on 170th Street, and lots of check cashing signs. The kosher butcher had gone and most of the stores were different, but Osherson's was still there. My mother liked the new customers. Even though she spoke only a few words of Spanish, she found the Puerto Rican customers much easier to deal with than the Jewish ones.

It was a short trip home across the George Washington Bridge. My parents had an apartment on the 10th floor of the Regency, 2150 Center Avenue. My mother was terrified to move, but once she did, she was ecstatic.

The doorman at the Regency was named Morris; he was very friendly. The building's lobby was enormous, like the big hotels in Miami Beach. There must have been twenty chandeliers hanging from the ceiling, all crystal and gold. The lobby had alcoves with soft Italian cream-colored leather sectional sofas, potted palms, sleek tinted glass and stainless steel end tables, and apricot and chocolate colored velvet and suede pillows casually strewn about. There were mirrors on every wall and on the ceiling. The elevator was completely mirrored with accents of antique gold and deep polished dark wood. The lobby and the elevator were redecorated every five years.

In 2007, three years after my mother died, I was teaching a meditation retreat for the Institute for Jewish Spirituality at the Garrison Institute. Garrison is housed in a huge stone monastery situated on the Hudson River right across from West Point. I went for a walk after lunch. It was a cold and windy day in late fall. The path was covered in golden orange leaves. I arrived at a ledge overlooking the river, which was steel blue-gray and flowing fast. Little white bubbles were playing hide and seek. The Hudson River was making its way to the ocean all the while sharing its grace, nurturing power, and love. I thought of my mother and how she loved the Hudson River. It made her so happy to live so close to it. From the balcony of the apartment in Fort Lee, she could see the tollbooths and the traffic passing over the bridge, but not the river. My mother knew it was there and that gave her enormous joy.

Some years after my parents moved to Fort Lee, my father died, I got divorced and moved to Philadelphia, and my mother learned to drive at the age of 70. She inherited my father's huge grey Oldsmobile. By now the store was closed and my mother invested her talents and passion in volunteer work in the local Jewish community, especially in the North Bergen County Hadassah chapter, and in her new friendships.

One day I got a call from her. "Sheila, I want to buy you a fur coat."

"That's very nice, Ma, but I do not really need a fur coat, or want one for that matter."

"No" she says, "you don't understand. Paul has this man in his congregation who is making fur coats for us at wholesale prices. We need to go into the city and measure you."

"Mom, I really do not think a fur coat would work for me. No one around here has a fur coat. It's just not me."

"Honey, that's okay. All you have to do is give me a time when you can come into the city to be measured. I am getting one and so is Lorraine. You will love it. It will keep you warm. Don't be like that. Someone wants to buy you a fur coat, you take it!" My mother did not raise her voice but her intensity was escalating.

"So let me know the next time you can come in and I will tell Paul. By the way it is a raccoon coat."

I had a lot on my plate. I was in rabbinical school. I was in a relationship with a man that was not going very well. I had two little kids and a lot of residual bitterness with my ex. I had a job. I had a women's group. I had political commitments. I was almost a vegetarian. And now my widowed mother was determined to buy me a raccoon coat.

I knew in every cell of my body that I did not want this coat. I also knew that I did not have the energy to oppose my mother. I knew she wanted the best for me. I didn't think I could explain to her why I did not want a raccoon coat. The river was too wide. I made the appointment. We went into the city to the workshop of my brother-in-law's congregant. I got measured. I got the coat.

The coat weighed about 25 pounds and felt like a suit of armor when I put it on. It was warm but it felt crushing. It came with a super-strong hanger, and I hung it in my daughter's closet. My kids called it Rosco the Raccoon. We thought of it as a pet. It was hard for us to have all these dead raccoons hanging in the upstairs closet. I only wore it once or twice in Philadelphia. Once I was out to dinner with some other rabbis and rabbinical students. One of the recent graduates had decided that she wanted to be a veterinarian after all and was enrolling in a vet school. "Sheila," she said, "can it be that you are wearing a raccoon coat?" I had to think on my feet. "Oh, no. You know these fake furs are made to look pretty realistic these days."

I wore Rosco when I came to Fort Lee, to please my mother. I looked better to Morris the doorman and to my mother's friends and the other people sitting on the Italian leather sofas in the Regency lobby. I looked better in the elevator with all the mirrors.

When I took a pulpit in Amherst, Massachusetts, I realized there was no way I would ever wear Rosco in the streets of this politically correct college town. It would be unwise and perhaps unsafe. I decided to give Rosco back to my mother. On the same trip when I picked up my father's torah, I left behind my raccoon coat.

My mother's great love for me was concealed in the gift of the raccoon coat. She wanted me to be warm and safe and to look more elegant and cared for than she feared I was. I wanted to please her, to receive her love, but not at the risk of losing myself.

Where is God? God gives me the strength to lovingly return this gift to my mother. This is the dance of the generations, the conversation with my mother that does not end in death. When understanding and forgiveness are revealed, God is present. God's love is greater than the love of my mother. It sees beyond the lobby at the Regency, beyond my being single, too thin, or too fat. It embraces every conflict and paradox. It sees into the depth of my heart. It knows that I am created *b'Tzelem,* created in the Divine image itself, of infinite beauty, a pure soul.

One Lone Purple Tulip, Mexico, December 2006

One lone purple tulip sits in the white onyx vase we
bought in Puerto Penasco.
In my mind I can see the nearly empty patio and the café
next door where we had lunch.
They forgot to leave out the meat as we asked.
I see the store crammed with onyx objects of all sizes and
shapes—lamps and ashtrays, bowls and coasters.
I can feel the desire to own something; and the limiting
desire not to spend money, nor to increase my
possessions, nor to indulge passing desire.
And here it is now on the dining room table,
So plain and beautiful,
A veined white opaque vase.
All one see sees is the top of the stem and one flower, a
purple tulip.
Maybe I should call it plum.
It's getting harder to see with these eyes.
I remember my mother struggling with her eyes when
she was old.

Discovering Meditation, Barre, July 1990

The first year I was sober I reconnected with Ed, the boy I'd known in high school, the guy I went to the senior prom with. He was in love with me back then, but I was looking for someone more edgy. I thought of him after 25 years and wondered what had become of him. Maybe I was ready for him.

Ed was divorced, a professor and a father of two boys. He was still very handsome, and I loved his blue eyes. Miraculously, we felt like home together. He was still in love with me but this time I was okay with that. Soon after we reconnected, he was diagnosed with kidney cancer. He told me I didn't need to stay with him now because that was not what we bargained for. I thought the opposite. Why had I come back into his life except to give him the love and hope he needed to fight the illness and to triumph?

We read Bernie Siegel's *Love, Medicine and Miracles*. We knew Ed would be an extraordinary patient. He was, and he died. I was completely overwhelmed with grief. He died two days after the first anniversary of my sobriety and a day before Abby's high school prom. I was held through the pain by friends and strangers and by my own ability to pray that I had found in recovery. I also went on healing retreats at Kripalu with the yogis and the Abode of the Message with the Sufis. There was no comparable Jewish place in those days. Or maybe I just wanted to do the healing away from the Jewish places where I was known and recognized as a rabbi, someone who helped others but didn't need help herself.

Months later I got a note from two friends from B'not

Esh urging me to consider applying for the job as rabbi of the Jewish Community of Amherst. The only thing I knew about Western Massachusetts was Kripalu. I loved the idea of being near the beautiful mountains. I was open to moving on, away from the place of my mourning. My daughter was in college and my son was ready to begin high school. It was time for a change.

Ezra and I came up to Amherst for an interview. I loved quaint New England in snowy December. The head of the search committee was an exuberant sprite of a man named Ted Slovin. Aside from being a founder of the synagogue, he was also a board member of Insight Meditation Society (IMS). "You realize, Rabbi," Ted told me, "that we are down the road from one of the premier Buddhist meditation centers in the country. What an opportunity for you to have this resource for your own spiritual renewal! Amherst, you understand," Ted said in his dramatic way, "is midway between Kripalu and IMS." I was curious about meditation.

I arrived in Amherst in the summer of 1989. The following summer I registered for a ten-day retreat at IMS, taught by Christopher and Sharda. My roommate was not respectful of the vow of silence and enjoyed schmoozing. I also had a friend who invited me for two long chatty walks during the retreat. Otherwise I was alone with my own mind. Sitting, walking, sitting, walking, eating, doing my yogi job (pot washing), sitting, walking, sitting, walking. Finally evening arrived and Christopher or Sharda would speak, giving me some relief from my own mind. Then sleep, dreams, getting up early and beginning again. The sitting was painful. My back, neck, and shoulders hurt most of the time. Much of the time, I felt sleepy and distracted and could not pay attention to the directions. I felt hopeless, useless, inferior, a fraud as a spiritual person.

Despite all of this, the teachings were incredible. It felt as if the teachers had been in my mind throughout the day. Their words created a sense of spaciousness. The process of returning again and again to the simple object of attention—the breath, the step, the pot I was scrubbing—expanded the dimensions of my mind. All the painful thoughts, the judgments, the fears, the endless desires for this or that to be different loosened their grip.

I understood that the teachers were teaching Buddhism, and the stories they told and the texts they quoted came from that tradition. At IMS, however, it was always very clear that no one was interested in your becoming a Buddhist. This was critical for me. As the days unfolded I started to translate the teachings into a Jewish spiritual language. I understood that the Buddhist reference to suffering, craving, and the conditioned "I" that always wants attention and amusement was equivalent to what Judaism refers to as false gods and idolatry. How indeed could I recognize and weed out idol worship from my heart? How could I end suffering? How could I heal the wounds that forced the walls of separation to be erected that kept me from myself, others, life itself, or God? How could I see the transient and the fleeting and distinguish that from the eternal and enduring? How could I deal with my own destructive habits without destroying others or myself? How could I recognize what is fantasy and what is truth? What are the stories that rule my life? How do any of us do any of this? These are Buddhist questions, Jewish questions, recovery questions, human questions.

I am moved by the practice of mindfulness. My entire being is engaged. I see how the stories in my mind proliferate. I see that when I allow my attention to rest on sensation in the body there is dynamism, change, and instability. Things loosen up. I am less a victim. I open myself to the infinite power of pure awareness, the light of presence. I open to the nameless energy of life that just is. I open to compassion. In Jewish language, I open to God's love, the power that heals, forgives, comforts, and through the pure act of presence ultimately transforms. I see infinite references to this process of liberation in Jewish prayer, in the texts of Torah and in the practices of a Jewish life. I experience how hatred and contention lock in an experience and deepen suffering. I understand through attentive patience and self-honesty that the more open I am to what is arising in this moment, the more balanced and clear is my mind and the more able I am to make wise and compassionate choices. The more *shalom*—wholeness or peace—is created, the more *tikkun*—mending the shattered and divisive nature of reality—is achieved.

I experience spontaneous lines of Jewish prayer rising in my heart that mirror my own inner sense of liberation.

How goodly are your tents, O Jacob
Your dwelling places, O Rebecca.
Make me a sanctuary and I will dwell in your midst.
The Eternal dwells in the midst of the storm.
The winds rage and home is not shaken.
Fear, desire, hatred, delight, success, loss—all come and depart.
The home of the soul stays luminous and embracing.
Windows open
Doors open
Curtains blowing in the breeze
Foundation in the center of the universe
In the flow of timelessness
In the eternity of love and compassion
Chesed v'rachamim.

The teachings and the practice of mindfulness become part of my life. They serve to inspire, sustain and strengthen me. I begin to teach mindfulness to Jews using the language of Jewish story and symbol. The key factor is that people are given a chance to see for themselves the nature of their minds, to know impermanence personally, to see the insubstantiality of the separate self, to experience the interconnection of all beings and to know viscerally both the causes of suffering and the end of suffering. Mindfulness practice contains the same principles that have always moved me. The principles are easy to articulate and difficult to practice. I ask myself, in this moment, to tell the truth, to be engaged with a community of seekers and practitioners, to keep returning to my intention, to develop tolerance for the other, the different, the unknown, the unpleasant, the frightening, to develop curiosity and a keen desire and ability to listen. Listen! Listen! *SHMA YISRAEL*—Listen up, Israel!—is the passionate Jewish affirmation of unity and interconnection.

Mindfulness gives me a new lens with which to interpret and understand the sacred teachings of my people and more deeply apply those teachings to my life. To what end? To live with more awareness, more compassion, more wisdom and more love. I discover that I cultivate wholeness when I learn to pay awakened attention without pushing away, grabbing, or fleeing. This leads me to a contentment that transcends the vagaries of changing phenomena, the contentedness of the psalmist who wrote: "*Ashrei yoshvei vaytecha*"—"Happy are those who dwell in Your House." The house of this body-mind and the house of life in this complex human reality and the house of this struggling planet can all be embraced when we sit down and partake of the infinite clarity of awareness.

Ashrei Yoshvei Veytecha

Just to take our seat and enter fully into this moment is
to recognize that we are part of something so much
greater than ourselves.
Happy is one who sits in Your house.
Ashrei Yoshvei Veytecha.
We relax into this moment remembering that we do
not possess this house: this moment, this body, this
world. And that makes it all the more precious.
In the simplicity of returning again and again to this
breath, this sensation, this sound, we are practicing
happiness.
The happiness of peace and contentment,
The happiness of feeling connected,
The happiness of greeting the sun in the morning or just
taking another breath,
The happiness of knowing that this bad mood will pass
and this harsh thought has no substance,
The happiness of letting go of ill will for this moment,
The happiness of allowing desire to come to its natural
end in the mind,
The happiness of growing still,
The happiness of seeing life and death in everything and
not being afraid.
Is this political? Well, I think it is.
This happiness doesn't hurt people we do not know.
This happiness doesn't tell us to be ashamed of growing
old.

This happiness doesn't tell us we aren't okay but can fix that if we try hard enough.
This happiness doesn't attract a lot of buyers and sellers.
It calls for careful cultivation like a field of precious jewels
Moment after moment.
It calls for dedication and community and willingness and faith.
It calls upon wisdom and courage.
It is itself a child of goodness.
So simple.
So huge.
But it is the only happiness there is.

Barton Poole, Summer 1992

I am on retreat. It is the middle of the summer. I am taking ten days out of my vacation time to practice meditation in silence. This is not the first time I am here. It is a very peaceful place. The trees are lush this time of year. Occasionally one hears a car moving down the street. The buildings are made of stone and it is cool inside. The meditation hall is comfortable. I can sit on a chair. The food is delicious, simple vegetarian fare with lots of fresh produce, homemade bread, and salads from the garden out back.

I am delighted to be here and to have some peace and quiet. My life is very hectic. There have been non-stop bnai mitzvah, meetings, classes, weddings, people in the hospital, counseling sessions, and public appearances. I am exhausted, and I know that these ten days will renew my spirit. I am thrilled that I do not have to talk to anyone except for a 10- or 15-minute check-in with one of the teachers every few days. I am delighted that no one will talk to me, tell me their problems or ask me for my advice.

It doesn't bother me that this is a Buddhist place. I would go to a Jewish retreat center if one existed, but here, no one cares if I am a Buddhist or not. I love the wisdom of the Buddha, the way it is taught here. It speaks to my heart and keeps me balanced during the silence when disturbing mental and emotional states arise. I have no problem translating Buddhism into Jewish language, a sort of religious simulcast. I make time every day for a long period of personal prayer with my *talit* (sometimes *tefillin*) and prayer book. I am often so touched by the old Hebrew prayers that I find tears running down my face.

The first night on retreat I notice one of the other participants, a man in his early 60s, tall, slender, gray-haired, restless, full of energy. He reminds me of President Bush (the first). This guy looks both incredibly uncomfortable on retreat and like an entitled, rich white Christian male. I take an immediate dislike to this man. I can't figure out why on earth he is on this retreat.

Whenever Mr. X comes into view I notice that feelings of aversion arise in me, followed by unpleasant judging thoughts. I have never spoken a word to this man, but this does not prevent me from disliking him and everything I decide he represents—especially power and arrogance.

As time passes, my mind clears. I see what is going on. I realize that I am the one who is suffering each time my mind moves into the contracted and separated place of ill will. The benefit to my sense of self is feeling superior to this stranger. I accept that my mind is creating a drama. There is no reality here, except that certain conditions have set off a chain of negative experiences. It is actually quite unpleasant. Once I see this, I can be compassionate with my own mind. The awareness itself dissolves the unpleasantness. It too is just a passing phenomenon. It moves along as long as my mind isn't fabricating more reasons to fuel the narrative. "George," as I begin to call him, becomes a minor figure in the retreat as other material takes his place.

On the last day of the retreat there is a sharing. There are about a hundred people on retreat, all sitting in a circle. For the first time we can see each other's faces. Each person has a chance to say a few sentences. This is our first speaking after 10 days of silence. I am nervous. I hear my heart thumping. I try to listen to what other people are saying. I am thinking of what

I am going to say. When it is my turn, I say: "This has been great. I am the rabbi in the synagogue in Amherst (less than an hour from here). As amazing as this may sound, I truly feel that my coming on this retreat makes me a better rabbi. In my experience, the dharma, the practice, this place is a life-line to the One, which I call God. I am very grateful."

A few people later it is "George's" turn. He looks so different when I am looking at his face. It is broad and open and there is a twinkle in his eyes. He says, with a very thick Southern accent, "My name is Barton Poole. I am from northern Mississippi, and I have a lot in common with the rabbi." He drawls the word "rabbi" out into at least three syllables. Now I am listening. "I am a Methodist minister and I feel that this practice gives me a chance to truly walk the walk of Jesus. It helps me live the message of the Gospels. I am very grateful."

Barton Poole and I look for each other in the dining room at the end of the retreat. We embrace. We have lunch together and talk. He tells me about his ministry, his Jewish daughter-in-law, his love of the dharma. I tell him about my shul and my kids and Maynard and the work I hope to do. We are like *landsleit* who have discovered one another. We share the dream of bringing the teachings of our traditions into our lives and the lives of our people. We both hope to wake up in this life and to transmit that possibility to others. We know how hard it is to see through delusion in our own minds and how any teaching can be corrupted and distorted. We have no need to be rivals; there is so much work to be done. It is a holy moment.

Barton Poole, my soulmate, is hidden in a man who reminds me of George Bush. Because there is some mindfulness and patience, the immediate aversion releases. Ignorance reveals itself. The mind jumps to false, sometimes ridiculous, conclusions based on scant evidence. When the mind has a little stillness, quiet born of time and space and practice, I am able to see through delusion. I see the thick material of the cloak become transparent. I realize, "There is nothing here worthy of my attention. Where am I right now? Oh, yes, this step, this breath, this sound of a bird singing." When I return to this moment, God is waiting for me, no longer covered in layers of confusion or judgment or old limiting stories.

Jack Rabbit

Jack rabbit, brown, sleek
Dashes across the dry grey earth
So fast
I hardly see where he comes from or where he is going
Like thoughts of ill will, greed and delusion
That seem to arrive from nowhere
Rushing toward endlessness.
Let them dash across
Free, unbridled, barely seen.
I hardly see where he comes from or where he is going.
Hardly?
Truth to say, not at all.
He comes from the past.
He is rushing to the future.
Neither exists.
With red dry eyes, burned by the desert wind,
I pause,
Right here.
I see him
Now
And only now.

The Rabbi Has Shoulders, June 19, 1994

Our wedding took place at the Jewish Community of Amherst where I was the rabbi. It seemed like the obvious place to hold it.

I liked the idea of a wedding in a synagogue. Our friends and family could come up to Amherst for the event. We held it in June after Ezra returned from his post high school year in Israel.

I knew a million rabbis but Rebecca was perfect for this ceremony. Maynard had no experience with the renewal of Jewish spirituality and creative rituals. He was not a synagogue attendee or a religious Jew. He was a Marxist sociologist, a secular Jew, and a humanist. Rebecca was capable of walking the perfect line. She also understood the essence of our relationship, and this was important to both of us. I invited my brother-in-law Paul to co-officiate with her. They were as different as can be, but cordial and cooperative.

The major issue was the invitations. Could I invite certain congregants and not others? Should we invite everyone to the reception or everyone just to the ceremony? There were people in the shul to whom I felt really close. Were they my friends? If they were, why couldn't I invite them to my wedding? On the other hand, where should we draw the line? Offending someone was a real risk, but when you offend your congregants, you offend your employers. Rabbis face this all the time. It was confusing, and I was in agony. Finally, we settled on inviting all the congregants to the ceremony and none of them to the dinner, which was at the University of Massachusetts and just for out-of-town guests. The board was gracious and put on a lovely reception at the shul for all the people in our congregation. Only one congregant made an appointment with me the week after the wedding to tell me that she was really hurt that she was not invited to the reception at UMass.

Maynard and I were funny under the *chuppah*. When we read the *ketubah*, we had to hold it at arm's length because neither of us could see without our glasses. Together, we were 99 years old; he was 51 and I was 48. Under the *chuppah* we were both crying and we had only a tiny piece of a tissue between us. Abby and Ezra, Maynard's son Aaron, and his niece Deb held the *chuppah* poles. The *chuppah* was my rainbow *talit*.

My 86-year-old mother was radiant at this wedding. She was tremendously relieved that I was finally getting married and she liked Maynard. She was in top form. Her black hair was well coifed and she wore an expensive satin and lace bright tourquoise dress with a straight skirt and high-heeled shoes to match. Slowly she walked down the aisle on the arm of her brother Louis and stood on the *bimah* during the ceremony, poised for her part: reciting the last and longest of the seven wedding blessings, in English. It was the honor she was due.

She stepped up to the microphone with deliberate, measured steps. She paused and eyed the crowd. She smiled as though she was running for office. When she spoke, it was a cross between Hillary Clinton in Madison Square Garden and Ethel Merman in "There's No Business like Show Business." Every word rang clear and loud, no need for amplification. She beamed. I was suppressing a laugh, from pleasure at her pleasure. We had expanded the traditional text in a few places; where it usually says "the jubilant sound of the young," we changed it to say "the jubilant sounds of the young and the old." My mother took about a minute to savor the word jubilant in her mouth.

Thanks to Rebecca we included a lot of political stuff in the wedding, which made Maynard comfortable. She included a powerful ritual of spilling drops from the wine glass to signify the incompleteness of our joy because same-sex couples lacked the right to marry. Ten years later I finally got to sign many marriage licenses for same-sex couples in Massachusetts.

Before the wedding, I had to decide what to wear. I decided to go shopping at a bridal store with a friend. I didn't want to spend a fortune but I did want to look like a real bride. I think that was because I was the rabbi. I didn't want to be the rabbi at my wedding; I wanted to be the bride. So I found a comfortable white lace dress, knee-length in front and longer in back, with sleeves that could be worn off the shoulder. I had orchids in my hair. No veil, no *kippah*, no *talit*. Very girly.

There are two aisles at the JCA. Maynard and I came down at the same time, each one in our own aisle. As I walked by, I heard someone whisper to her neighbor, "Oh, look, the rabbi has shoulders."

I am a rabbi. Being a rabbi, a male prerogative until this generation, conceals the fact that I am a woman. I want to be a rabbi. I want to be a woman. It is hard to be both. I don't know how to do it. How am I supposed to know? No one can teach me or tell me. I buy a wedding dress that reveals my shoulders. It is funny. God is laughing. Maynard loves me as a rabbi and as a woman. There are a lot of us now—women rabbis. God is happy!

Dancing at Camp, Summer 1996

When Ezra was 21 years old, he invited me and Maynard to visit him at camp to watch him lead Israeli folk dancing on Friday night and to spend Shabbat together. I was thrilled and put it on my calendar months in advance. A few weeks before the visit, Ezra called me and said, "Dad might be at camp the same weekend you are going to be there."

Influenced by my practice as well as my own preaching and teaching, I thought to myself, "Maybe this is the time for some healing. Maybe I can be calm enough to be in the same place at the same time with Steve without hostility or competition. There have been enough ruined graduations and traumatic family occasions."

Thursday night, before we left for camp, Steve called and said: "I have to be at camp on Friday night. I am very involved with the running of this camp. Could you plan your visit to arrive on Saturday morning instead?" There is a pregnant pause. How to respond? With indignant anger? With rage? With cynicism and sarcasm? With resignation and silent resentment? Somehow, another voice rises up. In calm tones I responded, "It is really important for me to see Ezra dance and this can only happen on Friday night. More important than that, I really want you to know that there is nothing I want from you. There is no need for you to change or to do anything differently. Therefore all that remains for us is the present. In the present I am totally fine to be with you at the same place and the same time getting a lot of *naches* watching our son." Another long pause. He said, "I was not expecting this. Let me think about it. I really did not think you would say something like this."

We all showed up at the camp on Friday night and made small talk, Steve and his wife and Maynard and me. We chatted with the other's partner and watched Ezra dance. He was fantastic! It wasn't totally easy and relaxed on the inside, but we were cordial and polite on the outside. Later that night I found myself weeping as we drove to our motel in Allentown. I recalled the years of blaming, resenting, competing; years of anger, superiority, and hatred. The well of tears felt infinitely deep for the pain we had caused our children.

I allow myself to feel it fully, and a bitter taste fills my throat. Tears wash down my cheeks. A silver stream makes its way to the ocean of forgiveness.

Family Reunion, The Catskills, Summer 2001

I thought of a quote from Yitz Greenberg as we drove up to the Catskills for a family reunion. It helped explain why I have stayed connected to the Jewish people and their story for all these years. He wrote: "All of Judaism can be summarized in four words, 'the triumph of life.'" This is not mere theology or metaphysics; it is visceral. Belonging to an ancient tribe makes this flicker of light on the great horizon, my little life, part of a big story with a grand purpose.

Maynard, Ezra, Abby, and I arrived at the Nevele Hotel, a slightly run-down resort a few hours from New York City. My mother's mother's family is a microcosm of recent Jewish history. About fifty people gathered, ages 3 to 87, coming from Argentina, Israel, Canada, and the U.S.—Massachusetts to Texas. The Australian branch sent their regrets. We were all descendants of Chizhe and Chayyim Aryeh Luria from Novodvor, a shtetl in what is now Poland (then it was Russia) near Bialystok.

Chizhe and Chayyim had five children who survived to adulthood: Itche, Shoshe, Fruma, and the twins, Velvel and Maishe. Itche, Yitzhak, the eldest, an ardent Zionist, left for Palestine in the 1920s, taking his children, already fluent in Hebrew. His son Ben Tzion, "son of Zion," now dead, kept a lifelong pledge never again to leave Israel, even for a short trip.

Shoshe, the oldest girl, went to Palestine in the 1930s with two of her children and two grandchildren. Two other children stayed in Poland and were murdered with their families by the Nazis. Her fifth child, Sortche, immigrated to Canada in 1938.

My grandmother Fruma was the youngest daughter of Chayyim and Chizhe and the first in the family to leave Bialystok. In 1906, with her two-year-old daughter, she set sail for America to join her husband and his family in New York.

The youngest boys in the family were twins. Velvel immigrated to Argentina and Maishe to Australia. Both married and had children.

Chizhe and Chayyim's descendents stayed in touch over a century of wandering around the globe. In another culture or time, we would likely be an extended clan living near each other. We would be each other's intimates, forming a web of relationships. But this is not that time or culture. We are dispersed.

My talented and loving Aunt Adele, married to my mother's brother Louis, got the idea to establish a family e-group and put out a call for a reunion. Many of my relatives responded. Others sent photos electronically and warm greetings.

At the reunion, one of the cousins brought a family tree blown up to 30 feet that covered the wall in our common room. We shared our stories with each other, showed pictures, reminisced, laughed, cried, and ate for a magical, intense, emotional weekend. During breaks, when we wandered through the lobby, we noticed other people in tearful embraces. Multiple reunions were going on simultaneously at the Nevele.

My cousin Avi was there, the one I met that long-ago night in Petach Tikvah, with his wife and children. He was a wealthy and successful psychologist living in Houston, Texas.

Tears in her eyes, my cousin Joyce excitedly showed me a

small black-and-white picture, taken in 1938 in Woodstock, New Brunswick, Canada. My grandmother's niece Sortche had just arrived from Bialystok with her teenage children Sylvia and Chayyim. My Uncle Louis took the picture. In it are my grandmother Fruma, her husband Sholom (Samuel Osherson) and my sister, Lorraine, who was only eight years old. My uncle had driven his parents up to Woodstock from New York so that my grandmother could see the first flesh-and-blood relatives she had laid eyes on in more than 30 years, her sister's daughter and grandchildren. Joyce showed the picture to Sylvia, now an 80-year-old grandmother living in Ottawa. Sylvia remembered the day as if it were yesterday.

At breakfast on Sunday, the conversation turned to "where and when do we meet again?" Yaakov, from Tel Aviv, almost 70, tall and erect, a former El Al pilot and retired manager and world traveler, immediately suggested Jerusalem as the obvious next site of our gathering. The Israelis were all enthusiastic. But one by one, the Canadians and Americans began to demur. "We're not that comfortable taking our kids there with what's going on." (It was the middle of the second Intifada.) Yaakov, undaunted, had another idea. "What about Bialystok? It would be amazing." Some eyes lit up, imagining the journey into the past together, the drama of returning. Yaakov was two years old when he left Bialystok, but Sylvia had been 14 and remembered. Now she tightened her lips and narrowed her eyes. "Never do I want to step foot on that land. I would not go back to see the graves of our people. Those murderers!" When Yaakov heard her response, he brought up Jerusalem again. Someone else suggested Canada.

We didn't talk about politics, religion, our careers, or our opinions. The stuff that our individuality is made of seemed to recede into the background, or perhaps we intuitively knew enough to stay away from anything that could divide, wound, or fracture the momentary sweetness of our reunion. Reunion—reunited—together from the root. We wanted to celebrate the survival and flourishing of this particular tree with its bountiful and fruitful branches rather than to dwell on the peculiarities of this or that leaf. We longed to savor the comfort of feeling so at home with one another. These few hours felt like a safe harbor in the turbulent story of our people. We gave each other permission to celebrate our being together. It felt like a triumph. Then we went our separate ways.

Leaving Israel, July 30, 1997

At the very end of my sabbatical, I waited at Heathrow Airport for my flight on British Airways from London to Boston. I had arrived a few hours before on El Al from Tel Aviv after spending the previous six weeks in Israel. My time in Israel was the climax of the seven months' break, invigorating, challenging, infuriating and inspiring. Now, waiting for my flight, I drank a cup of tea and read from the thick notebook which was the second half of the journal I kept during the sabbatical. Dreaming about Jerusalem, I wrote these words:

I am in a place where I have been forever
Where the dust blends into my skin
The smell of jasmine gets me high
The noise doesn't frighten me
And all the children remind me of my own.
The wounds never form scars in this miracle mountain
Piled high with pink and golden stones
Little parks filled with yellow roses and crimson
bougainvillea
Remembering lost parents and children weaving through
alleys and streets.
Empty fields ringed with infrequently collected garbage
and thorns; stray black and white kittens forage and
thrive.
No manners needed in this town.
Opinions loud as diesel engines.
Frantic readings of God's truth

Men rush to pray
So sure they know His will
Women bargain for tomatoes and chickens,
Carry heavy bundles and bellies and herd dirty children.
God's will, too.
Only the tourists seem calm.
Vacant eyed.
In awe or numb?
Buying gifts, eating ice cream.
Otherwise, Jerusalem is an earthquake, a volcano, no man's land, the valley of rebirth, the vale of rage, the destination of every God lover and mad man.
Jerusalem, you break my heart.
I pray for you.

After I wrote these words it was almost time to board the enormous plane, which took a while. When we finally took off, the BBC world news was on the large screen at the front of the cabin, with pictures of frantic scrambling. I heard the screams of terror. There had been a suicide bombing in the Jerusalem open air market, Machaneh Yehuda, that morning, leaving 16 dead and nearly 200 wounded. I had left my apartment less than an hour before the explosion. That apartment is next to the market.

Buffet in Eilat, March 2002

Abby and I met in Newark at the El Al terminal. We were flying to Israel to visit Ezra, 27, who had been living there since December 2000 in an "urban kibbutz," sharing an apartment with a group of idealistic twenty-somethings from the U.S. and Great Britain. Abby was 32 and living in Philadelphia. Neither of my kids had partners.

Abby and I had missed Ezra terribly and had planned this trip for a while. It was not a good time to go; the second Intifada was in full swing. As we got on the airplane, I said to Abby, "After this, no one will doubt our great love for our Ezra or for Israel." Tourism was almost at a halt, except for the Evangelical pilgrims.

Things were very tense in Jerusalem. Ezra invited me to lead a meditation session for his housemates on Saturday night. They opened the session to some friends from the youth group, and the room was pretty full. The young people sat around on couches, stools, and pillows. I gave my usual rap about meditation and why it is helpful. I explained how it is consistent with Jewish ideas and practices. I gave some instructions for sitting meditation and we sat for a few minutes. I taught walking meditation and opened up to some questions.

Then the sirens started. At first, we all ignored them. There are a lot of sirens all the time in Jerusalem—police, fire, bomb squads. But this was different. They didn't stop. Someone got up and opened the window and we saw rows and rows of fire engines moving up the street. The session abruptly ended and the room emptied. The young people went downstairs and asked neighbors, "*Ma kara*? What happened?" They turned on the TV and already there was coverage; the smoke had not yet cleared. Just up the street, maybe four blocks from where we were sitting, Café Moment had been hit by a suicide bomber. There were many casualties, dead and wounded. My heart raced. Ezra had gone Israeli dancing and still wasn't home. Had he stopped for a coffee? Everybody's mind was racing, thinking who might have been there, all feeling under attack. I mentioned to one of the girls that maybe Ezra went out for coffee. "No way," she said. "He wouldn't spend money in a café." A short while later he came home to find us all silently glued to the TV screen. There was nothing to say. Politics made no sense right now; the situation was too raw. These young people, after all, were choosing to make their life here.

The next day, Abby, Ezra, and I took the bus to Eilat. We thought it would be nice to go somewhere warm, have a chance to swim and relax. We were pretty sure that Eilat was out of the range of the Intifada.

Israel is a small country and Eilat, which is at its southernmost tip, is only about four hours from Jerusalem. We had reservations at a large hotel, along with a lot of Israelis who were in Eilat with the same idea. It wasn't as warm as we hoped, but we could still swim, snorkel, shop, and walk around without fear. The hotel rate included breakfast and dinner. The first morning we were psyched for an Israeli buffet breakfast. We handed the maitre d' our vouchers and he led us to a table by the window overlooking the pool. The restaurant took up two huge rooms, with hundreds of people of all ages and sizes darting toward the buffet and returning balancing plates piled sky high. All along the walls, the buffet tables were groaning with food: ten kinds of herring plus lox, mackerel, sardines, filet of this and that fish; ten kinds of white cheese, some salty and some not; yogurt and sour cream, yellow cheese, omelets, scrambled and boiled eggs; tomatoes, cucumbers, peppers, tuna fish, mayonnaise dips, melon, prunes, figs, olives and dates; cereals (hot and cold), vegetables, noodles, rice kugels, quiche, borekas, knishes, Danishes, bagels, hard rolls, soft rolls, crackers, muffins, sponge cake, and honey cake; every kind of juice, jam, marmalade, butter, margarine, and (of course) milk, tea, coffee, and cocoa.

I said to my adult children as we prepared to make our way to the buffet, "Okay guys, you know the drill. Take breakfast and lunch. Just pick up a few extra things for sandwiches so we don't have to buy lunch later."

My daughter looked at me and smiled. "Mom, what would happen if we just ate breakfast now and when we get hungry for lunch later, we buy a sandwich or a falafel or something?"

"But we always do this."

"I know. That's why I am asking. It feels like a hoarding mentality. How can I get the most for my money? How can I not be a *freyer*?"

"*Freyer*" is a popular Israeli word. It comes from Yiddish. A *freyer* is a loser, someone who is taken advantage of, someone who doesn't get their money's worth or what is coming to them. A great amount of energy is spent trying not to be a *freyer*. My mother would never want to be a *freyer*. Abby was asking me to relinquish that energy and just eat breakfast.

Ezra chimed in, "I am open to this, Mom. What do you say? Let's take the risk; let's splurge. Just eat what we want for breakfast and walk out empty handed."

I noticed that the people at the table next to ours were scooping piles of cheese and rolls into a plastic bag they had brought for this purpose.

I noticed that I was not eager to comply with my children's wishes. I was holding on to doing it the way we have always done it. I noticed the constriction in my face and chest. I practiced mindfulness of sensations. I noticed the tension in my body. It eased and I smiled. This was an opportunity to practice a tiny renunciation, a small bit of generosity. Could I do that without judging my neighbor, who was in hoarding mode? Wow, now *that* was advanced practice.

"Okay," I said. "Let's go into the unknown. Enjoy your breakfast."

I can't say it was easy but it made me happy to know I was free. I could choose to do something other than the habitual thing. It made me happy to please my children, even if it made me a *freyer*.

A Missionary to the Eskimos, Briarcliff Manor 2003

The Institute for Jewish Spirituality, where I teach mindfulness and yoga to rabbis, cantors, educators and lay Jewish leaders, ran a contemplative kayaking retreat in Alaska, which I participated in for two summers. We spent a week in a remote bay in southeast Alaska. A lot of the time we spent in silence, but we prayed and celebrated Shabbat and learned about this part of the world, the ancient rocks, the salmon, the whales, the Sitka spruce, the sacred web that holds us all. This is a fragile part of our endangered earth. Our spiritual work with Jews called us to make these connections.

I told my mother that I was going to be in Alaska for work on a meditation kayaking retreat. When I got home I sent her a picture of myself wearing a green Polartec shirt and green nylon pants and sitting at the flap of our tent, looking tanned and vigorous. I knew my mother would enjoy seeing me look healthy.

The next time I visited my mother, she was living at Brandywine Adult Home, a big old house with dark furniture and high ceilings that looked a little like a haunted house. It was actually set on Sleepy Hollow Road. It was a step down from her previous assisted living home, Atria, where she had lived for several years. Here she could get more care, which she had come to need. But she still ate in the dining room and had a social life with the other residents.

When I came, I found her sitting in the front lobby dozing. I came over and gave her a kiss. As soon as she saw me, she perked up and smiled. She was wearing her checkered blazer and beige polyester slacks. Her hair had turned grey; she stopped coloring it after her last boyfriend, Jack, died a year earlier. She told me then, "I am finished with men." She was 95 years old and looked thin and very small, and she couldn't hear unless you screamed.

Last year I told her that I was leaving the synagogue. She wasn't happy at all. "That is a big mistake, Sheila. Do you have any idea what you are doing?" But then, she hadn't been happy when I first told her that I was going to rabbinical school: "You will never find a husband if you become a rabbi." When I told her I was leaving Steve, she said, "Don't be ridiculous. Men are all the same, but you still need one." But every time, she eventually got on board, coming to visit me for the high holidays and watching me on the *bimah*. She found it bewildering, but she saw that the people liked me and I seemed to do a good job. She enjoyed schmoozing with my congregants and they liked her as well. Most of all, it was steady work. I had money to send my kids to college and buy my condo. Miracle of miracles—I found a lovely man to marry even after I became a rabbi.

Now, when I visited her, she said, "Let's go for a walk on the patio." "Okay, Mom." She pulled herself up and held onto her walker, which had a little wire basket in front where she kept letters and postcards, Lifesavers, a white lace hanky. I noticed that she had the picture of me in Alaska in the basket. It was hard for her to walk; every step was slow and labored, reminding me of the walking meditation on the retreats. One must pay close attention to every sensation of shifting weight, lifting, placing each foot. Once again, I was surprised by how short my mother had become. We didn't talk much. I told her about my kids and Maynard. I didn't think she really heard what I was saying, but she pretended to. The house had a large back lawn, where my mother liked to watch the birds and the flowers. We got to the end of the patio and turned around: time to come back in.

She went back to her chair, and before long one of the residents came walking by. My mother called to her, "Doris, come over here." "Good morning, Ida." Doris looked younger and sturdier than my mother. She had curly white hair with a lot of pink scalp showing. "Doris, I want you to meet my daughter, Sheila. I told you about her."

"Oh yes, of course. How nice. You have a visitor. Wonderful to meet you." She held out her small, warm hand to clasp mine.

"Ida, is this the daughter you were telling me about who is a missionary to the Eskimos in Alaska?"

My mother turned to me and said: "I was telling her about your work. Going to help the Eskimos become Jewish."

Doris said goodbye. I said: "Lovely to meet you as well."

She moved on. There wasn't more to say. I was glad my mother had her own way of understanding what I was up to these days.

Windfall, Tebenkof Bay, Southeast Alaska

Tiny things.
Are they fighting or making love?
A tiny spider spins a web between two stalks of grass.
Then the wind comes and it holds on tight.
So much more gossamer in this world than my eyes can
ever see.
A big thing.
"So where's the Zen garden?" I ask at Malibu, the sandy
shore where we get out of the kayaks.
Kurt says: "Over there. It's really nice. Check it out."
Then I see it.
The tree growing out of the rock and I find myself in the
crevice of the rock.
Place of infinite mercy and love.
I know it is my mother and me.
And our parents' parents and children's children.
All the way as far as it goes or will go.
Who knows?
I know it is God's way.
Trees grow out of rocks.
In every moment.
And I weep.
Big tears from the belly.
Then it's gone.

Rocks

Rocks grow out of critters who live in the ocean.
And trees grow out of rocks and critters eat trees and we eat critters and critters eat us.
And oil comes from critters. And we're using up all the oil. And Rosh Hashanah is coming. The world's birthday.
And kelp grows up to three feet in a day
And the tide uncovers and recovers eight feet of this island every day
And Kurt caught 60,000 pounds of sable or black cod in one day
And the earth is 4.5 billion years old
How odd, amazing and blessed to lose this critter and her endless chatter and just belong.
The rocks are perfect for idols.
I want to build an altar or bow down and worship one, any one of these rocks.
My ancestors said, "You can't worship one rock or even many rocks even though you can worship The Rock who is not really a rock but the essence, the swirl within all rocks, trees, otters, whales, salmon, people and stars."

Stellar Blue Jays

We are sitting together in the grove of ancient Sitka
spruce and hemlock branches a lattice in the sky
above.
Sitting in silence.
Breathing.
Last morning.
Closure.
Yael sitting at the base of the thickest tree, leaning back.
Then the Stellar jays come.
Blue.
And one particular bird starts to come closer and
squawk, sounding clear and croaky at the same time.
Sounding over the motors of the seiners in the bay
hoping for pink salmon.
The friends of the jays join the chorus.
Louder still
Kurt says: "I'll give you a translation of the sermon:
'Wake up!
See God in this world.
See God all the time!
In every thing, person, moment
And most of all, most difficult—says the stellar blue jay—
most of all in your self.'"
V'ahavta et Adonai
Love it all

Passover 1977/Amherst 2002

I started jogging when Steve and I were getting divorced. One day a friend of mine invited me out for a run. I couldn't believe how good it felt. My legs were weightless and my feet were walking on clouds. I loved it. At that time, I didn't know anyone who ran; running was completely new to me. I ran almost daily for 25 years. It did not matter where I was or what I was doing. I ran in Scranton, Philadelphia, Amherst, Jerusalem, on the beach, the highway, in the desert. I ran when I visited my mother in Fort Lee, in the middle of meditation retreats, on vacation, on Jewish holidays, on any terrain, up and down hills, in snow, rain, and 100-degree heat. I had to be really sick to take the day off.

I kept running after I stopped smoking, after I became a rabbi, after I stopped drinking, after I remarried, after menopause. Usually running was a solo activity, but sometimes I had a running companion. In the early years I ran some races but after a knee injury during a half marathon, I decided not to race, just to run.

I did other stuff while I ran. I learned the morning prayers in Hebrew by heart so that I could say them while I ran. I said prayers for the people I loved. I offered prayers to the people who passed me by whom I did not know. I said prayers for the difficult people in my life. This was very helpful during the year I had a conflict with someone in the synagogue. Sometimes I said prayers for myself, wishing myself safety, happiness and peace. This also helped.

I wondered at times whether running was an addiction or something in the service of the highest. It could go either way. Part of me needed to do it as a bulwark against the demon of fatness. Compulsive exercise does go with the distorted self-image of anorexics. I did not feel completely free not to run. If I missed a few days, I started to feel bad. On the other hand, it kept me afloat. I combined it with other practices that served my wholeness and well-being. It contributed to equanimity and clarity and made me feel good. I stopped starving myself and my periods came back. Running enhanced my life and the lives of those I touched.

Sometime in my mid-fifties my hips started hurting. Running seemed to make the pain worse. My back hurt and my knees had less give. First I tried to ignore the pain. Then I went to doctors, physical therapists, and chiropractors. I tried acupuncture. I had one goal: to keep running without destroying my body. One physical therapist was certain that I didn't need to give up running. I was in the process of making a huge decision about leaving the congregation in order to work more independently as a meditation teacher. I shared a vision of a future connection to the Institute for Jewish Spirituality, which was just forming. I needed the running to clear my head and to balance me. I complained to Maynard, "I don't know what to do."

When I started to teach meditation to rabbis at the Institute, Myriam Klotz, a rabbi and yoga teacher, started her yoga classes, which I took and enjoyed. She was doing Bikram yoga in Philadelphia. A friend of mine from AA was going to Bikram at a studio in Northampton. I started to go. The room temperature was 104 degrees. The practice was an hour and a half long, a set of 24 poses, exactly the same every day. I could do it and get the benefits of running without hurting myself. I enjoyed the heat and the sweating. It was time to tell the congregation that I would be leaving. It was time to give up running. I just knew it was.

It was hard to leave the synagogue and not know exactly

what I would do or who I would be, and it was hard to give up running. Every time I saw someone in little shorts jogging up the hill near my house, I winced. My cells craved running like chocolate. But I realized that while this activity once helped me, now it did not serve my well-being. It did not enhance the life force any more.

After I started doing Bikram yoga, my friend Nancy Flam invited me to her favorite yoga studio. Her style, Anusara, means "opening to grace." It blends precise alignment principles with an open-hearted devotional intention. It was not in a hot room. It is rooted in mindfulness and celebrates the divine beauty in each moment, in each person. It reminds me of the Hasidic teaching, "The whole earth is filled with God's glory." Posture work is the outer form. The essence of the practice is revealing the Divine splendor in each moment, in our very own minds and bodies. This is a teaching and a practice I could use. It contradicts all the old ideas of "not good enough." Could I believe that Divine goodness and light are accessible through this moment of awareness? Through this breath? I told myself, "You do not have to believe it. It is a practice." I still had to keep myself honest. I had to keep paying attention and to ask myself if yoga is becoming a field for competition, pride, judgment, or the excessive effort which devours playfulness. Am I trying to show off? Am I trying to prove something? What is true in this moment?

Miraculously, the space that was revealed in my life by leaving the synagogue gave birth to the Institute for Jewish Spirituality, which addressed the essential issues of leadership and spirit in Jewish life. Similarly, the space that emerged when I stopped jogging moved me into the world of Anusara yoga, a practice that goes to the roots of my being. It lovingly touches the shame and grief that surrounded my birth, the sense of unworthiness that shadowed my life as it impels me forward in my journey. Not only am I truly enough, I partake of divinity, infinity, pure goodness.

I naturally translate this into a Jewish vocabulary. Adam, the first human (all humans are encoded in the first one) is created *b'tzelem elohim*, in the image of the Divine. Yes, we all partake of Divinity!

There is a phrase in Torah that expresses for me the distorted thinking that often blocks the realization of *tzelem elohim*. It is in Deuteronomy and repeats the story of the 12 tribal leaders who scout out the Promised Land. Of the 12, 10 tribal leaders refuse to follow the Divine lead and enter the land. They say to Moses, "It is because the Lord hates us that he brought us out of the land of Egypt." I know the power of this view in my gut. It can be triggered by a casual glance or remark, a mistake, a sense of being excluded, a million things. It is so painful. Even though it is false, it still causes so much hurt. But I am being led into another world where this story is revealed as delusion. I am invited along with everyone else to step into my fullest manifestation of *tzelem elohim*. This is grace. I am grateful.

Benevolent Witness

It is not about changing myself.
It is about being who I am.
Sounds simple now.
After all the years of effort to become someone.
Someone else.
Someone better,
Someone with power and recognition
Someone more acceptable, more worthy,
I find out I don't have to be anyone else.
How nice! What a relief!

The Announcement, January 2006

I picked Abby up at Bradley Airport in my new dark red Prius, which she had never seen. I was thrilled to see her. It was January break for her in her master's program. I had only seen her three times since her wedding in June. She looked radiant. Her skin was clear and smooth and her long dark hair, which she wore loose, was shining. There was something easy and relaxed about her but I didn't give it any thought.

We drove to Florence, where I had a singing lesson. Abby agreed to come with me and meet Justina and hear me sing. Abby herself has a beautiful voice and loves to sing and lead services. When she was younger she was always in the choir and school musicals and she knows all the words to all the shows by heart.

But I'd never thought of myself as a singer. When I led services, I did my best but I always deferred to someone else and felt musically inadequate, as if the sound coming out of me was wrong and unpleasant. I was then teaching an intensive retreat program for cantors. Hearing the cantors sing together moved me to tears. I wanted to understand the cantors better, to learn how singing is a way of connecting to spirit, to God.

My friend Peg Stearn was studying with a voice teacher she adored and invited me to come to one of her lessons. Her teacher, Justina Golden, was a goddess, broad and bright, with golden hair, very dramatic. She might launch into an aria at any moment. She spoke in poetry. I came to class with Peg and, quite spontaneously, asked Justina if she thought I could learn to sing.

On my first day she told me, "I have a hunch that you have an unusually high voice. You have been singing low your whole life and that is why you haven't been able to carry a tune or feel comfortable. You have a magnificent instrument. Women are often told to restrain their high notes. It is another form of suppression and control. I love working with older women. There is nothing to be afraid of anymore and there is so much life to express." So I started taking singing lessons with Justina, having a grand time singing way up there. It sounded and felt really good to me.

Abby came to our session and heard me. She also had a chance to sing for Justina, who complimented her. We were all laughing and feeling great. Then Abby and I went for lunch to Miss Flo's Diner.

"Do you want to share a tuna fish sandwich and something else, Ab? They have really good tuna salad here."

"No, Mom, I am not eating tuna fish at the moment. I think I'll have egg salad."

"Okay, honey, that's fine. Whatever you like."

After lunch we went to Stop and Shop and bought groceries and odds and ends. We finally got to the condominium where I live. I got out of the car and took Abby's little suitcase out of the back. She got out of the car and came over to me. We were standing in the parking lot.

"Mom?"

"Yes, honey, what is it?"

"What are you doing next Rosh Hashannah?"

"Next Rosh Hashannah? Well I don't really know. It's only the beginning of January. We have time to think about it. I have no idea."

Abby and I had led services for the previous four years, since I left the synagogue, at Elat Chayyim, the Jewish retreat center in the Catskills. But we have pretty much decided that we are not going to go back.

"Mom, how would you like to babysit your grandchild next Rosh Hashannah?"

I am totally caught off guard. I am quivering. My mind is blank and blurred. Finally I scream!

"What are you talking about? Are you pregnant? Oh, my God!" The tears start to flow. I rush toward her and look into her beaming face.

I would turn 60 in March. For months, I had been thinking about a dramatic way to acknowledge this birthday, which felt significant. I looked at brochures about treks to the Himalayas. Now I know what this birthday would be about.

Thank you, Abby. Thank you, God.

"Yes, of course I will babysit on Rosh Hashannah."

And that is exactly what I did.

Naming Hadassah, August 2006

As soon as I finished teaching the IJS rabbis' retreat in Connecticut, I headed to Philadelphia. The Israeli army had invaded Lebanon; Israelis were evacuating the north. Haifa was being bombed. Israeli soldiers were heading for Beirut. The news was awful. Abby was due July 30, the day I arrived. Abby and Nathan had already moved out of their apartment in preparation for a big move to Ann Arbor after the baby was born. Nathan had just graduated as a rabbi and taken a job at the University of Michigan Hillel. They planned to head for Michigan when the baby was two weeks old. For now, they were living in a borrowed apartment belonging to rabbinical students who were spending the summer studying in Israel.

As the war worsened, the students decided to come back from Israel and Abby and Nathan moved into the house of a family that was in China for two weeks. We listened to the terrible news, watched Larry David DVDs, checked websites for baby carriers and cloth diaper systems, got invited to a lot of folks' homes for dinner, went for regular ultrasounds and acupuncture with Abby, and waited. The baby was born just as the kind family was returning from China and there was a ceasefire in Lebanon. Nathan and I, the doula, the midwife, and the nurse were at the birth. The midwife said, "It's a girl!" A few hours later, Ezra and I packed us all up and moved us to the home of yet another generous family in the neighborhood, which was spending the next two weeks in Cape Cod.

Abby and Nathan had decided that they were going to have a covenant ceremony naming the baby on the 8th day, the traditional day for male babies to be circumcised and named. Friends organized food and invitations. Abby and Nathan asked the rabbi of the synagogue to officiate at the ceremony.

Now there was the matter of the name. The parents did not want to discuss the name with anyone, least of all the grandparents. Abby and I had talked months ago about naming the baby, if it is a girl, for my mother. Abby had even asked me then what I thought about Hadassah as a name. Hadassah is the Hebrew name for Esther, the hero of the Purim story. This is a ribald fable that does not mention God; instead, human agents reveal God's saving love. Queen Esther/Hadassah is a Jew living in disguise in the palace until the moment is ripe to identify herself. She acts with tremendous courage to challenge her husband the king and to save her people. The Book of Esther, *Megilat Esther*, literally means revealing that which is hidden. Esther is a Persian name, cognate of Ishtar, but in Hebrew it means "hidden." On Purim, we read Esther/Hadassah's story and we wear masks. We hide ourselves behind fantasy faces to reveal what may otherwise remain hidden, even from ourselves.

So what does this all have to do with my mother, Ida Peltz? My mother became an active member of the Jewish women's organization, Hadassah, founded in 1912 by scholar and Zionist activist Henrietta Szold. Among its many worthy projects was the establishment of the premier medical institution in the Middle East, serving all people in that region, sponsoring youth *aliyah*, rescuing Jewish children in distress around the world, and numerous other humanitarian and educational efforts. My mother loved Hadassah. She was president of her chapter until she was 92. It gave her community, purpose, and recognition. Despite the occasional aggravation, it made her happy to be part of something greater than herself.

My mother always felt that her name, Ida, was measly. She

was not given a middle name like her sister, Lillian, who already had three syllables in her first name. She felt that Ida was a throwaway name for a second daughter. The song "Ida, sweet as apple cider" did not compensate. She felt that her Hebrew name, Chaya, was also very plain. She considered but then rejected the idea of changing her name to Iris or Irene, as some of her Ida-peers did. She was loyal to her given name, if not proud or fond of it.

Nathan was eager to name the baby after his Aunt Myrtle. She was his mother's aunt, a source of goodness and love in his family and a surrogate grandmother. Coincidentally, the English translation of Hadassah is Myrtle. Meanwhile, a beloved great-great aunt on Steve's side was also in the running. Even though I was not privy to the conversation I became completely attached to the idea of my granddaughter being named for my mother. The magnitude of the desire came with a proportionate amount of fear that this would not happen. I was having a very hard time not knowing.

No one knew the baby's name until the moment at the ceremony when the rabbi announced it. He himself was only told minutes earlier. He chanted to the crowd of more than a hundred people, in the very same room where I first saw a woman wearing a *talit*, "Her name will be called in Israel Hadassah Tikva bat Natan V'Avigail." Abby and Nathan explained that she was being named for her great-grandmother Ida and her great-aunt Myrtle. Tikva, meaning hope, signified the fact that she was born hours after the ceasefire in Lebanon, eight days earlier. It was a big name for a little baby.

When the baby was 13 days old, we headed off to Michigan in two cars and with whatever stuff had not already been sent, Abby, Nathan, the baby, Maynard, and me.

As If

It is true that life grows in its own time according to its laws and rhythms.
Spring comes after winter—not before.
The way things are can be observed
If one is quiet and patient.
The way things are can be appreciated
If one is willing and humble.
Still the mind loves to act "as if..."
As if it can make the rules
As if it can write the script.
Then, believing all the "as ifs," it is lost in a maze of pretense and pretension.
Again.

Conversation with my Mother, September 2006

I am walking up a mountain with my back to the retreat center, Spirit Rock. I am walking up to the first level. The sky is really blue. It's warm. I am starting to sweat. It's quiet; there is no wind. I come to level ground and the path turns and becomes steeper. I move around the level part. I start to climb the steep path. On my right is a twisted tree, a scrub oak, with thorns and small leaves, growing out of rock. I have seen this tree before. I need to keep walking. I pass a small bench. It's harder to breathe. I see there is a little more to get to the top. I push; I push; I stop. The view is vast. Gold grass, straw mountains, tiny houses on the other side.

My chest is heavy. I miss the baby. I wasn't ready to leave the baby. I miss my mother, who died right before my daughter Abby got engaged, about two and half years ago. "I need to talk to you, Mom. I need to talk to you." I am going down the hill. I feel tears in the back of my throat. My heart is so heavy and my throat is starting to burn. I feel silly to be in this kind of pain. Then I hear my mother's voice in my ear. It is unspeakably sweet, sweeter than anything I have ever heard in my life: "Sweetheart. It is so good to see you. Tell me what happened." "Mom," I am speaking to her now, "I have something so good to tell you. It's about Abby. I was there when she had the baby. She had a little girl and she named her Hadassah after you, Mom. Isn't that the greatest thing you ever heard?"

My heart releases. We are at peace.

Flying Home, October 2006

Flying Home after two months
Tired to the bone
Empty and full
In love with this new person
Taken over by life when I wasn't looking
Totally exhausted from the inside out
I am tired with all the generations of women saying goodbye to their offspring
Daughters leaving mothers and mothers leaving daughters,
Across oceans and continents.
I feel my mother saying goodbye to me.
How much I miss her
I didn't visit her enough.
When she saw me her eyes always lit up.
Somehow I missed it.
I was too afraid of being judged, molded, controlled, criticized.
I hope Abby's less afraid. I hope I am judging less.
Please God!!
Time for *Tashlich*. Casting into the clouds that float beneath us.
Clouds, take the fear and distrust—just leave the love.
The delusion of a separate self completely cracked open when that baby was born.
I am mother, daughter, grandmother and none of them. Porous skin, diaphanous, substanceless, light as

air, as clouds. This doesn't belong to me. This is not about me. This me has no beginning and no end.
This is life lifting.
This is God being God.
L'Chayyim.
The spheres twirling in spirals, cells joining and separating,
Light years and stars
Changing places in time and space.
Above the planet at 35,000 feet
A tail wind.
"Excuse me, would you like something to drink?"
Flying home.

Hadassah's First Birthday Party, August 2007

Naomi Newman writes that "fall down get up" is one word. Even immersed in a life of commitment to training our minds and hearts, we still falldowngetup. We make mistakes; we lose it. That is the nature of being human. It is hard and humbling.

This event took place eleven years after the visit to the camp to watch Ezra dance. In those years, Steve and I were blessed to attend two graduations, two weddings, and a baby naming, in peace.

I was on the telephone, talking to one of the rabbis I work with, when an electronic voice interrupted: "Mi-chi-gan." It was my daughter, calling unusually late. I finished my conversation and called her back at 10:20.

"Too late honey?"

"No-no-no it's fine"

"What's up? How you doing? How's everything?"

"Good, good. Everything is fine. It's okay. I have something to talk about."

It was late and I was tired. We'd only been back a few days from Mexico, where I realized I had Lyme disease, which was scary. I was put on antibiotics but felt weak, vulnerable, disoriented, frail, and old. Maynard had missed the bus in New Haven and wasn't home. Ezra was supposed to come that night but wouldn't be there until very late. It was dark. I did not want to hear anything upsetting.

I said, "Okay, tell me what's up."

"It's going to be difficult. Daddy is planning to come to

Hadassah's birthday party. You won't have that much of an overlap. He'll be here Sunday till Tuesday and you're coming Monday. Only two days."

I am swirling in my brain, in my body. I am holding on for dear life not to say anything, not to allow myself to bleed all over the phone. A live wire is exposed. Nerves, the bone, the muscle, the core of the place—I am squeezing as tight as I can just to say, "Is it definite?" I am barely breathing.

"Well, I sent out the e-vite and he got it and he decided to come."

"Is he coming alone?"

"Yes."

"I thought you were going to see him the week after the party at the wedding on the West Coast? We have been planning this trip for a while. We're driving out. How are we going to both stay at your place?" The words start to pour now. I can't hold on anymore. I say: "Well, why are you calling me?" My voice is black with bile. It's inside my chest, coming up from the bottom of my throat. I know it is going to spill out. I am getting to the edge of the wave and she says: "I wanted to find out how you would feel about it." Her voice is very thin, but sharp, like a blade.

"How do I feel? I feel lousy." Then I hear my own voice. It is grim, contracted. "Well if he's coming, he's coming." Now there's a screech inside my voice. A hideous squeal. It's boring a hole into her mind and into my heart and out into the world and it is too late.

After that, the conversation did not get better.

In the end I said something to insult her father and she hung up on me and we tried calling each other back. Finally we reached each other and I apologized and she apologized. We didn't talk for the next 22 hours or so. I was weeping with rage. How dare he? How could he? Why me? Every negative pathetic victim-voice arose. Hadassah, my dear, our dear little sweetheart, our granddaughter's first birthday. She doesn't even know it is her birthday. I can find people in my mind to support my view that this is the most disgusting thing that anyone can do. He dares to come out there when it is my turn to be there? I am not going to share that space with him.

By the time Maynard finally got home, I had turned myself inside out. Exhausted, I cried myself to sleep.

The next day I talked to Ezra, who said, "What are the ground rules here?" He has a master's degree in conflict transformation. In the end I accepted that, yeah, of course, I have to share. This is my granddaughter's grandfather. What was I thinking? What are the ground rules? Up until now, since they moved to Michigan a year ago, each set of grandparents has visited one at a time. But for the last eleven years Steve and I have shared the big events in the lives of our children. The wires got crossed, and a hydrogen bomb went off in my head.

Why do I still get triggered like this? Yes, I'm not feeling loved, I'm not feeling strong, I'm not feeling good, I'm not feeling seen. All of these are not even feelings. They are old, old thoughts of competition, fear and inadequacy that weaken me. All the spiritual practice in the world does not save me from this falldowngetup moment. It is a human moment. I wish it had been different but it wasn't.

There are stories in the Torah that sometimes present themselves spontaneously in my mind as templates for stories in my life, and this is one such moment. I am reminded of the story of Moses ascending Mount Sinai to receive the Torah. He is with God at the summit for forty days and forty nights. Meanwhile, the impatient people below make the golden calf. They are unable to endure Moses' absence or receive the magnitude of God's transmission. Moses and God see what is happening. God indicates the desire to destroy all of Israel and start from scratch with Moses and a new nation. Moses calms God's wrath and proceeds down the mountain. When he gets close to the scene of revelry and idolatry, Moses smashes the tablets, God's own work, thereby voiding the covenant. Moses acts swiftly; the calf is destroyed, Aaron is confronted, and the people are severely punished.

The dialogue between Moses and God continues. Moses begs God for a direct and personal revelation. Moses is hidden in the cleft of a rock on Sinai, as a mysterious manifestation of God passes by. In that moment, God's thirteen attributes of mercy are pronounced. God's essential attributes of love, patience, and kindness are stated in human terms. Forgiveness, too, is revealed as a quality of the divine.

The Biblical account concludes with Moses ascending Sinai again to receive a second set of tablets. These tablets are carved by Moses and written by God, unlike the first set which were purely God's workmanship and writing. Moses returns after another forty days. The Biblical account does not supply dates for any of these events. The rabbis felt compelled to put the narrative in history and link these dates with the Jewish calendar. Shavuot, mentioned in the Torah as the festival of first fruits, becomes the day of the giving of the Torah, the first tablets. The rabbis assign the second ascent of Moses to the mountain top to the first day of the month of Elul, the beginning of the late summer period of reflection and return. Forty days later is the tenth of the month of Tishrei. This is Yom Kippur. This is the day Israel receives the second set of tablets. These are the tablets of the renegotiated marriage that repair and restore the relationship. These are the stone slabs that heal the betrayal, the disappointment, the anger, hurt, and punishment.

There is a tradition that says that they all dwelt together in the Holy Ark, the whole tablets and the broken pieces.

I imagine what this might be like on the inside.

The fear, the greed, the envy, the judgment, the hunger, the rage. All these jagged slabs—the wanting, the bragging, the dreaming, the impatience, the intolerance. They are all here in a human package, along with the courage, the love, the generosity, the energy, the joy, the wisdom, the tenderness. All here, all mixed together: a human being. But the broken bits have no enduring substance and turn to dust, while the whole tablets become the ark itself, contained in and containing all.

Life seems to me to be a series of opportunities to let go of the expectations and stubbornness that block the way to forgiveness. This is how I understand the line in Psalms: "God's love endures forever." I am comforted by the realization that there is always a way back. I know that falldowngetup is one word. Falling down is not a failure; it is part of learning to walk. Each time I experience the transformation of forgiveness (never yielding the equal truth that every action does have inescapable consequences) I stand for a moment in the bright light of God's essence.

Steve did not come to the birthday party, but it would have been all right if he had.

That's The Way It Is

That's the way it is
When it snows and then rains on top of the snow and the
rain freezes
And then the snow melts underneath
And you go crunch when you walk
As the thin layer of ice cracks underneath.
And that's the way it is
When the skinny branches of the saplings that were just
planted last week
Turn into crystal sticks.
And that's the way it is when the hardiest of the oak tree's
leaves,
Brown and tough,
Still hang on, not ready to yield
Like the old ladies and an occasional man,
Who sit waiting, with my mother, brown and tough,
In the parlor, where she lives.
And that's the way it is when I fill up with sadness, fear,
hurt, sick of being human
And then the river overflows
And it is quiet again.

Our Hands, October 2007

I spend time looking at my hands in yoga poses, especially downward facing dog. The placement of the fingers is important. The wrist creases need to be parallel to the front edge of the mat. Both sides of the finger pads need to be strongly rooted. Index finger points straight ahead. Even the knuckle pads, a segment of the anatomy I hardly ever noticed before, need to press firmly into the ground. All of this attention to alignment helps reveal the power and energy in the body. Our teacher says, "Yoga is the effort to align with grace." This could be the definition of any spiritual practice. In another setting we might say, "the effort to align with God."

My hands are bony. Rivers of blue veins crisscross the knuckles to the wrists. My hands are speckled with brown freckles and pale spreading spots that one starts to get as one gets older. I think they call them liver spots. Maynard calls them old people spots. My fingers are long and thin. When I was younger people always said, "You should play the piano."

My mother's hands were soft and smooth. Her fingers were neither slender nor stubby. I always thought they were perfect hands. The palms of her hands were like feather pillows. I could sink my head into those hands. We would sit together and hold hands. We walked and held hands.

My mother loved Abby's hands. She was always saying, "You have such beautiful *hentlach* (little hands)." Abby's baby, Hadassah, had those precious pudgy dimpled baby hands that were busy, busy, pointing or grabbing or stuffing something in her mouth. She was all curious, all learning. Who knows what her hands will be like when she grows up?

I see my mother counting the cash at the end of the day in the back of the store. That was a sacred time during which she could not be interrupted. My mother's hands always got black from the counting. The money was put in a special brown cloth bag with a very heavy zipper and a lock. This was called the "depo" meaning the deposit. I never understood what that meant but I guess it was deposited in the bank after hours.

Once when my mother was close to 70, she was held up at gunpoint in the store. Two men wearing black wool hats and masks over their faces entered the store when she was there by herself. My mother said, "We have nothing to give you. Just take whatever is in my purse. There is nothing in the cash register." The taller one said, "Look, lady, you better not lie to us. We killed an old lady like you last week. We don't give a damn about killing you." She opened the cash register drawer and sure enough it was empty. She didn't tell them that the depo was in a rear drawer, where she put it every night before dropping it in the bank's night slot. The telephone rang. The men panicked, turned, and left the store.

When I was sixteen my Jewish youth group had a project to collect money for Israel. It was called BSB, which stands for Building Spiritual Bridges. My mother and I came up with the idea of crocheting *yarmulka*s and selling them for a dollar each at chapter meetings, camps, or conventions. My mother taught me how to crochet. We used thick wool so the work went quickly. My mother found leftover yarn from sweaters she had knitted over the years and unraveled an old shawl of black yarn with silver speckles, and we crocheted two dozen *yarmulkas*. She asked other relatives and friends for old bits of wool. She was a demon crocheter. Her silky hands flew as she spun out *yarmulkas*, striped ones, purple and pink ones, multicolored in shades of green or blue or rainbow shades. We learned how to put a Jewish star in the middle.

I had bags of *yarmulkas* to sell. My mother's hands were busy every moment there was no customer in the store.

My mother's hands could fix anything—rugs, skirts, or dresses that were too short or too long. Zippers were her specialty. These smooth round hands could get in there and make the crooked straight.

I remember going home from the store with my mother. It was dark. It was winter, and the street was slushy. Cars were passing by. We waited at the light at the corner of Walton Ave and 170th Street. As she did every time we crossed a street, my mother took her hand to my neck. She gripped my neck as a way to hold onto me and steer me across the street. I felt the tension in her body. I felt it in my neck and down to my stomach. She was not holding my hand. She was holding my neck. She felt safer that way, negotiating the terror at every corner. Years later, it is still hard for me to cross a busy intersection. The cars all look like they are ready to run me over. Once in Cairo, I lost the entire group of people I was with because I froze in terror at the crosswalk.

It is Friday night. The store closes early, at 6 pm. My mother is home. She has koshered and boiled the chicken and made the soup on Thursday night. She takes a square white paper napkin and puts it on the divider between the kitchen and the dinette. Then she puts the stainless steel tubular Shabbat candlesticks on the ledge made by the divider and puts the stubby white Shabbat candles in the holders. Taking a match, she lights the candles. Those soft, frightened, tender, capable, tense, loving hands wave in front of the light and cover her face. She says the blessing. She looks into my face, smiles and says: "Gut Shabbos."

When my mother lived in Atria, an assisted living facility with a small Jewish population, every Friday afternoon there was a Shabbat gathering, sometimes led by volunteers from the local synagogue, sometimes by one of the Atria male residents. My mother took this group on, becoming the self-proclaimed president of the shul. She recruited for the service among the Christian residents, promising them real wine and chalah. She enlisted my Aunt May, my father's younger sister, also living at Atria, to be her assistant and to hand out the prayer books. May was never a shul-goer but she could not resist my mother's authority. My mother had the official job of lighting the Shabbos candles. Those same soft hands, now thin and frail, waved away the week and brought in the light.

I am visiting Hadassah's nursery school. It is Friday morning and we are going to gather for "Shabbat." All the different age groups crowd together on carpet squares in the lobby of the Ann Arbor JCC. Hadassah is one of the "Ducks," the under twos. Older children are kangaroos, bunnies, frogs, etc. She is 14 months old and she sits on my lap. The leader begins by lighting the Shabbat candles. Hadassah takes her chubby pink little hands and holds them in front of her face. She is completely merged with the moment, the light, and the prayer. Then comes the little plastic cup of grape juice and finally the chalah. "Chalah" was one of Hadassah's first words. All week long she talks about Shabbat and chalah. Every time she sees a candle flame she covers her eyes with those little hands.

I buy Hadassah a Shabbat kit. It is a set of brightly colored plush objects: a golden-brown chalah, a set of candlesticks with orange plush flames, a Kiddush cup and wine bottle (with purple plush at its mouth) and a dark red velvet chalah cover. Hadassah spends hours playing with the Shabbat set during the week. She covers and uncovers the chalah and pours the wine. She stuffs the plush things back into the plastic purse it comes in with those little hands. "Shabbat" she says when she calls on the phone. "Shabbat Shalom."

Ida would get such a kick out of it.

Shiviti Adonai L'Negdi Tamid *(I Place God Before Me Always)*

May I take a moment.
May I take a moment to rest right here.
To feel my breathing
To sense aliveness
Inside and outside.
May I take a moment.
To feel the beating of my heart.
To sense the air on my cheek.
To hear the sounds that come and go,
To smell the air.
May I take a moment.
To rest
To open
To listen.
And to remember
that I am
connected to everything
that is,
was and
will be.
Shiviti Adonai L'Negdi Tamid
May God's life-giving presence be known in every part of my body, in the depths of my being and in everything I encounter.
In this moment.

Glossary of Terms (from Hebrew unless indicated)

Aliyah Immigrating to Israel; literally ascending

Avinu av harachaman Our father, father of mercy

Bnot Esh Daughters of fire

Chesed v'rachamim Loving kindness and compassion

El Malei rachamim God, filled with mercy

Hagba The honor of raising the torah scroll after it is read publically

Kaddish Prayer in Aramaic recited by mourners

Ketubah Written marriage contract which is part of a Jewish wedding

Kiddush Prayers usually said over wine or grape juice on Sabbath, holidays and special occasions

Kippah Skull cap—also called *yarmulka* in Yiddish

Landsleit In Yiddish—folks from the old country

L'olam ulolmei olmeia Aramaic words in Kaddish meaning forever and ever or to the very ends of time and space

Minyan Jewish prayer quorum of ten adults

Naches Pleasure in the accomplishments of those close to us

Shacharit Jewish daily morning prayer service

Talit (sometimes pronounced *tallis;* plural is *talitot*) Jewish prayer shawl

Tashlich Ritual on the Jewish New Year when bread crumbs representing our sins are cast into a body of running water

Tefillin Small black leather boxes with sacred scrolls that are tied around one's arm and forehead during certain prayer services

V'ahavta et adonai You shall love the Lord

Yarmulka In Yiddish—skull cap

Acknowledgements

I am grateful to my cherished and amazing colleagues at the Institute for Jewish Spirituality (ijs-online.org): Rachel Cowan, Nancy Flam, Jonathan Slater, Myriam Klotz, Marc Margolius, Margie Jacobs, Pat Fettinger, Sadie Rosenthal and David Cavill. Rachel encouraged me to write from the beginning. Nancy was part of the writing group with Andrea Avayzian, "Rabbi-Rabbi-Rev," which gave me loving support.

Thanks to Ted Slovin, my spiritual friend.

Deepest gratitude to Sylvia Boorstein for reading and re-reading and for her always wise counsel and a great title.

Thanks to Jean Claude Van Italie who brought out the voice of the personal storyteller in me. Thanks to friends who have been on this journey with me: Bobbi Breitman, Rebecca Alpert, Rebecca Jarosh, Adina and Norman Newberg, Bob Stern, Judy Glaser, Kate Stevens, John Hoffman, Paula Green, Jim Perkins, Martha Ackelsberg, Judith Plaskow, Jeff Roth and Peg Stearn.

Thanks to John Clayton and David Breakstone for their thoughtful reading.

Thanks to the Barre Center for Buddhist Studies for inviting me into their calm and beautiful space to do this writing.

Thanks to David Eve for helping me with the computer.

Thanks to Linda Roghaar, Jay Elliott, Molly Wolf and Rebecca Neimark for making the manuscript into a real book!

Thanks to all the remarkable teachers of Torah, mindfulness and yoga I have known.

Thanks to all my beloved students.

Thanks to Abby and Ezra for reading their *ima*'s stories, for their laughter and tears and for all the joy they bring into my life along with Nathan, Hadassah, Yehuda, Olivia, Aaron, and Erin.

I am deeply grateful.

Also by Sheila Weinberg

Preparing the Heart: Meditations for Jewish Spiritual Practice, (audio) Institute for Jewish Spirituality, ijs-online.org, 2005.

Breinigsville, PA USA
24 January 2010
231255BV00001B/2/P